Black Children
Their Roots, Culture, and Learning Styles

Black Children
Their Roots, Culture, and Learning Styles

Revised Edition

Janice E. Hale-Benson

The Johns Hopkins University Press
Baltimore and London

Johns Hopkins Paperbacks edition, 1986
93 92 91 90 89   8 7 6 5 4

The Johns Hopkins University Press
701 West 40th Street
Baltimore, Maryland 21211
The Johns Hopkins Press Ltd., London

Library of Congress Cataloging-in-Publication Data

Hale-Benson, Janice E., 1948–
   Black children.

   Bibliography: p.
   Includes index.
   1. Afro-American children—Education. 2. Afro-Americans—Social conditions. I. Title.
[LC2771.H34   1986]   371.8′2   86-45459
ISBN 0-8018-3383-3

This book is dedicated to my parents,

Cleo Ingram Hale and Phale D. Hale

Those who profess to favor freedom,
*   and yet deprecate agitation,*
Are men who want crops without
*   plowing up the ground.*
They want rain without thunder and
*   lightning.*
They want the ocean without the
*   awful roar of its waters.*
This struggle may be a moral one;
*   Or it may be a physical one;*
*   Or it may be both moral and physical;*
*   but it must be a struggle.*
Power concedes nothing without a demand.
*   It never did, and it never will.*

Frederick Douglass
August 4, 1857

—Excerpt from a speech on West India Emancipation, delivered at Canandaigua (In Quarles 1969, p. 354).

Contents

Preface to the 1986 Edition

Early childhood education, though still in its infancy, has contributed importantly to public recognition of how much young children desire stimulation and how much they are capable of learning. This sensitivity to the significance of child development has given rise to the "Superbaby" syndrome. In April 1983, a *Newsweek* cover story reported on this essentially white, middle-class phenomenon. Practitioners of it tend to be parents who have delayed childrearing until their late thirties. They are essentially two-career, affluent couples who believe that if you want a great career, you get out there and make one. And if you want a great baby, you get out there and make one. These parents are sending their children to prestigious preschools to which a two-year-old must have letters of reference and test scores in order to be admitted. Mothers are playing music to babies in utero so that they can learn to appreciate the classics. One-year-olds are being shown great art with the names of the artists on flash cards. They are likewise being exposed to the works and names of European composers. And six-month-olds are being taught to read—and are being taken to baby gymnasiums to work off baby fat. This alertness to the influence of the early years is almost becoming early childhood education hysteria.

It is very important that the Black* community be aware of this phenomenon, because many parents in quest of Superbaby have placed their children in private schools, have lobbied for legislation to obtain tuition tax breaks for private education, and have defeated school bond levies that support public education. The masses of Black children depend upon a strong public school system for their education. However, it is equally important for Black parents to become aware of the achievement gap between Black and white children and to assist the schools in helping Black children reach their intellectual potential.

---

*I capitalize *Black* throughout because it refers to a specific racial group, as does Caucasian, and is now replacing the less preferred *Negro*.

Howard Gardner (Ellison, 1984) suggests that Western social scientists have a narrow conception of what intelligence is. Most intelligence tests assess an individual's abilities only in the areas of linguistic and logical-mathematical intelligence. In his book *Frames of Mind*, Gardner describes seven ways of viewing the world. He believes that each of these ways is equally important and that, even if they do not exhaust all possible forms of knowing, they at least offer us a more comprehensive picture of intelligence than we have previously had.

In addition to linguistic and logical-mathematical intelligence, Gardner lists five more varieties. Spatial intelligence has at its core the ability to find one's way around an environment, to form mental images, and to transform mental images into physical ones. This intelligence can be expressed in visual art. Musical intelligence is expressed in the ability to perceive and create pitch and rhythmic patterns. Bodily-kinesthetic intelligence would be revealed in gifted fine motor movement, as seen in a surgeon, or gifted gross motor movement, as seen in a dancer or an athlete. Interpersonal intelligence involves understanding others—how they feel, what motivates them, how they interact. This realm of intelligence is expressed in social skills. Intrapersonal intelligence refers to an individual's ability to be acquainted with himself or herself, to have a developed sense of identity.

The intent of Gardner's work is to knock language and logic off their pedestal, to urge consideration of the range of human faculties in any assessment of intelligence and in efforts to develop human potential. This perspective should prove particularly useful in facilitating the development and achievement of Black children. A purpose of this book is to legitimate the study of Black child development. Gardner's analysis should assist us in identifying the strengths of African-American culture and the skills with which Black children are imbued. Heretofore, Black people, in the opinion of Barbara Sizemore,* have been made to feel ashamed of their strengths because they have been characterized in stereotypes. They then play "catch-up," trying to excel in such "white" areas of achievement as language skills. She recommended that we build bridges between the areas in which Black children seem to be "naturally" proficient, such as music, and in which we want them to achieve, such as mathematics—areas which seem to be related.

Gardner addresses the fact that Scholastic Aptitude Test and IQ test scores reward children who are able to give quick responses to short-

---

*Banquet address at the annual meeting of the National Black Child Development Institute, October 1975.

answer questions. In the short run these tests can predict the children who will do well in school. (I submit, though, that they do not predict as accurately those who will not do well.) However, he maintains that the tests do not have good predictive value for what happens beyond school, that there is only a modest correlation between scores on IQ tests and success in professions.

One can go beyond citing the elevation of language and logical intelligence as the primary abilities assessed by intelligence tests and can pinpoint ethnocentrism in the choice of which aspects of those abilities are assessed and which ignored. My father is fond of a saying that the Golden Rule is, He who has the gold makes the rules. This comes to mind when one considers which language skills are measured by assessment instruments. The myth that language is not valued in Black culture is used to explain why Black children do not score as well as white children on measures of language facility. The fact is that Black culture gives rise to highly charismatic and stylistic uses of language. The oratory and homiletics of the Black preacher are examples of charismatic language in Black culture. There is no counterpart in white culture to the oratory of a Dr. Martin Luther King, Jr., a Rev. Jesse Jackson, a Barbara Jordan (who, incidentally, is a preacher's daughter) or a Shirley Chisholm. The verbal rituals, particularly of Black male children, expressed in woofin', soundin', signifyin', chants, toasts, and playin' the dozens are examples of stylistic uses of language. These language skills of Black children are not assessed on the standard measures of verbal intelligence. Rather, it is the skills demonstrated by white children that are rewarded. "He who has the gold makes the rules."

It is incumbent upon Black professionals to identify the intelligences found especially in Black children and to support the pursuit of their strengths. We must also, as a community, begin to intercede for Black youth with those who would exploit their talents. Unfortunately, at one end of the continuum many Black youth are locked out of the mainstream; at the other end many are exploited by the music and athletic industries. We need to help a larger number of Black children discover and develop their several intelligences. We need to circulate the economic profits from Black talent through the Black community as many times as possible by gaining greater influence in those industries that market Black talent.

I have written this book to stimulate a different conversation and, I hope, a different research orientation toward the education of Black children. I am advocating that the subject be approached from the point of view of the cultural differences that derive from African heritage. I have pulled together the research and analysis of scholars who support this perspective. There are other approaches to and other points of view and conclusions about the genesis and importance of culture in the educational process. Many of these are not discussed or reviewed thoroughly in this or in the previous edition, although several are mentioned. This book is not intended to be a comprehensive treatment of ways to conceptualize Black culture or a comprehensive review of approaches to the education of Black children. There is evidence in the research literature for alternative explanations to the one set forth here. However, I have elected to develop the particular point of view contained in this volume. In the introduction to the first edition, I stated that the book should be regarded as a statement of a problem—a working paper. It is neither a finished, data-based theory, nor a curriculum, nor a "how-to-teach-Black-children kit." The first edition was an attempt to share an analysis of the then existing research literature that might contribute to a framework for such a theory.

The epilogue to this revised edition was written to add updated evidence to clarify my perspective. I have attempted to answer the questions raised by students, colleagues, and reviewers since the first appearance of Black Children, in 1982. Caroline Jackson, for example, suggested that I include in the epilogue a summary of the data that documents the achievement gap between Black and white children, since not all parents and educators are familiar with this evidence.

After discussions with scholars and educators throughout the United States, I felt that a fine tuning of my arguments as presented in the first edition was clearly called for. There have been many responses to my work, and several aspects of it have been misunderstood. I have addressed these challenges in the epilogue. A key challenge was whether a pedagogy for Black children as an ethnic group is called for. There seemed to be a need to go beyond the discussion of the social-class-versus-ethnicity question in chapter two of the first edition.

Prevailing "liberal" thought in America finds it acceptable to create "compensatory" educational opportunities for lower income children. If that group of children happens to be Black, there is no objection. However, there is an objection to the notion that Black children across socioeconomic boundaries would benefit from a distinctive educational process. Fortunately, we now have the data from the research of Jacquelyn Fleming (1985), which revealed that Black colleges do a better job of motivating and preparing Black students than do integrated schools.

Fleming studied 2,500 Black and 500 white freshmen and seniors at 15 colleges, including Spelman College in Atlanta, Ohio State University in Columbus, and the University of Houston. Her study was conducted over a seven-year period. She found that, even though the

Black colleges had very limited resources and many operated under severe financial difficulty, students at Black colleges gained more intellectually than did their peers at integrated schools. White colleges enroll more Black students nationally than Black colleges, but Black colleges graduate more Black students than do white colleges. In the epilogue, I call for more documentation of the reasons for the success of Black colleges in educating Black students. Such documentation would support provision of a distinctive educational experience for Black children at earlier ages.

A white educator said to me that white parents, as he sees it, do not object to Black children receiving a good education. They just want them to receive it in the schools as they presently exist. They object to changing the schools to accommodate the learning styles of Black children because they fear that such changes will have a deleterious effect on the achievement of white children. As I see it, then, Black children are caught between a rock and a hard place. Liberal thought is in favor of integration but not special entitlement programs. White liberals favor integrated schools but do not address the achievement gap between Black and white children in those schools.

In the epilogue, I go beyond the first edition to carefully delineate the fact that Black children across social classes are at risk in the traditional educational process. My analysis is that Black children must master at least two cultures (Black males must master three). In many ways these cultures are not congruent. Parents and educators must help children straddle these cultures and resolve intercultural conflicts if they are to achieve success in school and in the workplace. I believe that early childhood educators have a unique opportunity to assist parents in preparing their children to become bicultural as well as in creating responsive, child-centered learning environments.

Several of the reviewers of the first edition, notably Warren Simmons, suggested that I address some of the flaws and weaknesses of the African heritage theory of Black culture that is a foundation for my work. I have, as a result of his suggestion, deepened my discussion of the affirmative and negative theories of Black culture, giving the reader a more comprehensive picture of the issues that are being studied and debated in this area.

Another purpose in writing the epilogue was to include recently published research by scholars such as Hakim Rashid, Diane De Anda, V. P. Franklin, and Amuzie Chimezie. V. P. Franklin has persistently asked such penetrating questions that I have included his comments in the manuscript so that the reader can benefit, as I have, from our continuing dialogue.

Finally, I have written the epilogue to serve as a bridge between *Black Children* and my work in progress, "Facilitating Black Children's

Intellectual Development," which is designed to delineate a process for improving Black children's performance in school. I suggest ways to protect and nurture the self-esteem and ethnic identity of Black children while improving their reasoning, memory, language, creativity, and problem-solving skills. Most of all, since we have apparently been unable to correct the distortions of the intelligence-testing system, it seems to me that we must become savvier at preparing our children to excel in their performance on such measures as now exist.

Neither Black nor white people will be able to survive and achieve in this society if they are mediocre. John Dewey once said, "The education that is best for the best of us, is also best for the rest of us." We cannot allow Black children to be educated for mediocrity. On a test I took in college the scores for the class were As, Bs, and Fs. The professor's comment was, "Well, the class is clearly divided into those who know and those who don't know." Likewise is our society being divided. There is no longer a stratum in our society where mediocrity can be viable. That is why we have high school graduates doing the work that non-graduates did twenty years ago. That is why we have college graduates who are underemployed. We have to prepare all children for excellence because the mediocre will not be able to survive in our society.

It is also very important to assert that, as significant as the early years are, they are not the only significant years. Children need a good start, but Black children face several critical periods in their development. One such period seems to be the fourth and fifth grades when Black children experience a slump in their achievement. The adolescent years are particularly turbulent, and the young adult years are especially important for the opportunities they offer, which may determine the quality of later life.

My efforts and this book owe a great deal to the grassroots network of professional organizations, churches, and individuals who have supported my work. There has been a very silent network that has made this book our book. The first edition lacked benefit of mass media attention, highly visible reviews, or Madison Avenue marketing. Yet, to my amazement and the amazement of my publishers, *the community* has given this book life. Thanks to you for all of us.

I wish to express my gratitude to the Chairman of my department, Dr. Thomas W. Frew, and the Dean of the College of Education, Dr. Richard McArdle, at Cleveland State University without whose support this edition would have been impossible. Thanks also to Jane Kane for typing the manuscript. I am grateful to George Thompson, my editor at the Johns Hopkins University Press, for having envisioned this edition and for working tirelessly to make it a reality long before he shared the vision with me.

I would also like to acknowledge the support and friendship of my pastor and his wife, Rev. and Mrs. Otis Moss, Jr., pastor of Olivet Institutional Baptist Church in Cleveland.

I am grateful to Dr. V. P. Franklin, Dr. Sandra Scarr, and Caroline Jackson for reading the preface and epilogue and for their suggestions and comments.

Thanks to the "man in my life," my husband, Keith A. Benson, for his love and support.

Finally, I wish to reiterate the dedication of this book to my parents, Cleo Ingram Hale and Phale D. Hale, who provided the "desk" upon which I write and the potential for this kind of work.

Acknowledgments

This book was made possible by contributions from many people to my personal and professional life. I am indebted first to my parents, who put me together and hold me together. I am grateful also to Dr. Cecil Cone, President of Edward Waters College, and Dr. James Cone, Professor at Union Theological Seminary, who are my mentors and spiritual advisers. Next to my parents, they have made the most substantial contributions to my growth and development.

I thank my former professors in the Early Childhood Education Department at Georgia State University for the foundation they provided and for their continual support of my career, especially Dr. James Young, my adviser; Dr. Martha Abbott, my friend; and Dr. Joseph Stevens. I acknowledge the support and encouragement I have received from colleagues such as Evelyn Moore, Dr. John Dill, Dr. Asa Hilliard, J. D. Andrews, Dr. Robert Staples, Dr. Wade Nobles, Dr. Joseph McMillan, Dr. Na'im Akbar, Dr. Thomas Berndt, and Dr. Evelyn Gilliard.

I am especially indebted to Dr. William Hall at the University of Maryland, College Park; Dr. Michael Cole at the University of California, San Diego; Dr. Edmund Gordon at Yale University; and Dr. Sandra Scarr at Yale University for providing me the opportunity to study with them as a post-doctoral fellow. Their concern and guidance have made a critical difference in my career, and their thinking helped shape the content of this book. Others who contributed are the late Professor Charles Davis, Caroline Jackson, Dr. Vincent Franklin, Dwight Andrews, Dr. Sylvia Boone, and Drs. Edward Zigler and Sharon L. Kagan of the Bush Center for Child Development and Social Policy—all of Yale University.

I appreciate the support I have received from the administration of Jackson State University in assisting me to launch my research career, especially President John A. Peoples; Vice-President Estus Smith; Dean Beatrice Mosley; Dean Oscar Rogers; my department chairperson, Dr. Georgia Napier; and my colleagues, Dr. Winona

Williams-Burns, Dr. Boyne Coats, Dr. Betty Langley, and Dr. Lena Myers. Thanks also to my graduate assistants Ivy Lovelady and Burlene Brumfield for their editorial assistance, to Alice Singleton for typing the proposal for the book; to Linita Brumfield for typing the manuscript, and to Jimmy Young and Ivy Lovelady for the photographic work.

I acknowledge the support and kindness of my countless friends who have been supportive in general through the years but especially as I moved coast-to-coast pursuing post-doctoral study: Caroline Jackson, Monica Kaufman, Alveda Beal, Pamela Hoffman, B. J. Hampton, Dr. Gloria Walker, Angel Crayton, Patricia Coley, Tshaye Llorens, Brenda Stevenson, Ellen Pinderhughes, Dr. Mary Louise Serafine, Dr. Geraldine Brookins, Stella Davidson, Dr. Jeanne Middleton, Lynnette Shelton, Rae Dillon, Louise Jones, Sonja King, Dr. Rita Clark-Chambers, Janet Humber, Toni Humber, Dr. Warren Simmons, Dr. Denise Borders-Simmons, Dr. Carol Phillips, Gloria Brown, Dr. Ruth Robinson, Dr. Barbara Jackson, Denise Coles, Dr. Ronald McMullen, Dr. Anita DeFrantz, Dr. David Jones, Glenda Williams, Dr. Richard Middleton, and Mr. James Wade; my siblings, Marna Hale Pace, Hilton Hale, and Phale Hale, Jr.; my grandparents, John Ingram and Janist Preston; my aunt, uncle, and cousin, Dorothy, Raymond, and Ralph Grier.

I thank Dr. Pearl Dove and President Elias Blake of Clark College for the support they provided during the early years of my career. I am grateful for the leave of absence they granted that enabled me to pursue post-doctoral study.

I appreciate the friendship and encouragement from The Man in my life. He doesn't have to be named because he knows who he is.

Finally, I thank Louise Hanson, the managing editor of Brigham Young University Press, for her vote of confidence when she asked me to prepare this manuscript.

For permission to quote from their publications, I am grateful to the publishers listed on the copyright page.

1982

Foreword to the First Edition

The science of human behavior is in its infancy. Psychology, sociology, anthropology, sociolinguistics, and other related disciplines developed at the same time that Europe was in its ascendancy and was beginning to extend its political control throughout the world. Therefore, while Western behavioral science has developed in this environment, it has also served, frequently, as the handmaiden of colonial expansion and exploitation. This aspect of the development and use of Western behavioral science has been well documented by a variety of authors. Among them are Walter Rodney, *How Europe Underdeveloped Africa*; Chinweizu, *The West and the Rest of Us*; Franz Fanon, *A Dying Colonialism*; and Diane Lewis, *Anthropology and Colonialism*.

In addition, many authors have examined the use of Western behavioral science as a vehicle for political control within western nations. For example, R. Weinreich in *Hitler's Professors* and Allen Chase in *The Legacy of Maltus* have examined in detail the misuses of science in support of exploitation. While the politics of this situation is very important, it is the impact of the politics on the science of human behavior that interests us here.

Current difficulty in understanding Black children and how they develop in America is really only a part of the fallout from the historical pattern of development of Western behavioral science. For example, in its investigation of all the world's people, one of the chief characteristics of Western behavioral science has been a rigid ethnocentrism. The obvious problem created by this ethnocentrism is that information about human behavior becomes distorted. The problem becomes compounded as behavioral scientists examine the growth and development of African-American children. Since many African-American social scientists are trained in the Western behavioral science tradition, there is no guarantee that simply because a person is African-American he or she will see things more accurately. Similarly, it is not automatic that Europeans or Euro-American behavioral scientists are totally encapsulated by their past. However, the overwhelming predisposition of those who have been trained in the Western behavioral science tradition is to attempt to view the behavior of others through Western eyes. Therefore, the kind of scholarship displayed by Dr. Janice Hale is fresh, perceptive, and urgently needed.

Dr. Hale has proposed that understanding the African-American child is dependent upon a view of that child in the context within which the child lives and moves. One would think that this would be entirely obvious to scholars. Certainly, in the physical and biological sciences, every attempt is made to account for anything that would have an influence on the things being investigated. Environmental variables are meticulously sought out, examined, recorded, and analyzed; yet, in the behavioral science area, which has tried so hard to imitate the physical sciences, there is a consistent failure to attend to even the most gross forms of environmental variation among people being examined.

Dr. Hale has marshaled an impressive array of evidence necessary to support her discussion about the lives of African-American children. She is sensitive to the literature that examines the growth and development of the African child in Africa without the necessity of comparing that child to any other child. Further, she has incorporated into her discussion references to systematic study that demonstrate clearly the retention of elements from the African experience in African-American environments. Dr. Hale shows that the African-American child exists in a culture made up of African retentions and the American experience, with special attention to the fact that the American experience has included oppression for African-American people.

When it is established that many African-American families and their children experience a unique cultural configuration, it becomes important to include within the study of African-American children a perspective that comes from the study of culture and cognition. Abundant data show that culture patterns influence the way information is perceived, organized, processed, and utilized. Consequently, a discussion of the growth, development, and "cognition" of the African-American child must take into account that culture is one of the greatest environmental variables. It is at this point that Western behavioral science has failed in the study of African-American children. In order to illustrate that these points are not merely theoretical, Dr. Hale has summarized data about the play behavior of African-American children and has analyzed that data in order to suggest how cognitive style may be perceived through that play behavior. This cognitive style is an outgrowth of the unique cultural experience of African-American children.

As suggested by Dr. Hale, implications of her research are far-reaching. Approaches to education, mental health, family, community adjustment, and other areas can be informed by the kind of synthesis provided in Dr. Hale's book. Her work provides a model for those who would avoid the mistakes of the past. It is a model because it is an attempt to give appropriate weight to culture as the medium through which human behavior, for any group, can be understood. It is also a model that demonstrates how investigators of human behavior can take both a micro and macro view of the context within which human behavior occurs. If the frame for investigation is too minute, meaning is lost. Similarly, if the frame is too gross, meaning is lost. It is only through the integration of these two extremes, through a holistic perspective, that those who seek to understand the African-American child have any hope of success. Dr. Hale's work is a real contribution to this effort. It will prove to be of major value in the field of early childhood development and education.

Asa G. Hilliard
Fuller E. Calloway Professor of Urban Education
Georgia State University

Introduction

He who controls images controls minds, and he who controls minds has little or nothing to fear from bodies. This is the reason Black people are not educated or are miseducated in America. . . .
The system could not exist if it did not multiply discrimination. . . .
It is no accident that there is a blackout on the Black man's contribution to American history. . . .
An educator in a system of oppression is either a revolutionary or an oppressor. . . .
The question of education for Black people in America is a question of life and death. It is a political question, a question of power. . . .
Struggle is a form of education—perhaps the highest form.

—Lerone Bennett*

The American educational system has not been effective in educating Black children, as this book will substantiate. The emphasis of traditional education has been upon molding and shaping Black children so that they can be fit into an educational process designed for Anglo-Saxon middle-class children. We know that the system is not working because of the disproportionate number of Black children who are labeled hyperactive and who are being given drugs as tranquilizers—again, as this book will show. We know that the system is not working because of the disproportionate number of Black children who are labeled mentally retarded and placed in "special classes." We know that the system is not working because of the disproportionate number of Black children who are being suspended, expelled, and "pushed out" of schools. We can see that

---

*Excerpts from "The Challenge of Blackness," a speech delivered at the Institute of the Black World in Atlanta, Georgia, in 1972.

the system is not working in the high Black teenage unemployment rate and the overrepresentation of Black people in the prison population.

The orientation of American social scientists has been to define Black home environments as pathological and Black parents as deficient in preparing their children for school. This underlying assumption has precipitated the development of numerous compensatory education programs designed to ameliorate the effects of growing up in Black families.

The orientation of American educators has been that Black children need the exposure that comes from being educated with white children. Therefore, there has been an attempt to achieve a racial mixture in the schools by busing children away from their neighborhoods. This plan has been received with hostility by most white parents. It has received a mixed reaction in the Black community. Many Black parents remember the "separate-but-equal" doctrine that relegated Black people to separate schools that were grossly inferior in the educational background of the faculty, the quality of the facilities and materials, and the length of the school year. These parents feel that if Black children attend schools with a predominantly white population, they are more likely to enjoy the advantages that will be assured for white children. Other segments of the Black community object to the implication by proponents of busing that something about a Black child sitting next to a white child will enhance the achievement of the Black child.

During the sixties concern grew in the Black community about the type of Black person being produced by the American educational system. The perspective of Carter G. Woodson (1933) was reiterated. He wrote that Black people have been "miseducated" into confusing their interests with those of the dominant society. The Black community indicted the American educational system for attempting to socialize Black children into accepting the history, culture, value system, and behavioral patterns of Anglo-Americans. Black people needed to maintain a clear identity of themselves as an oppressed people if they were going to be able to make a contribution to the struggle for liberation. The liberation struggle is long-range; therefore, the educational process must serve a consciousness-raising function that will prepare Black people to make a contribution to a struggle that began centuries before they were born and that will extend for centuries after their deaths.

In response to this concern, many "alternative schools" were created during the sixties to address the issue of education for struggle

Has the American educational system been effective in educating Black children?

and identity. These schools were concerned with ideology, culture, and values and with defining and implementing "Black education." That education is important.

However, this book is addressed to the issue of the eighties: education for survival. This facet of education is the *tooling* function of education. We must address the facts not only that Black children are not being effectively educated but also that they are being "miseducated" in the schools of this nation. Black children must achieve competency in mastering the tools of this culture if they are to survive. It is not enough to wear dashikis, speak swahili, and eat "soul food" in educational settings, as desirable as those activities are. We must create an educational system that not only celebrates African and African-American culture but also imbues Black children with the skills they need to survive in this society and to contribute to its creative development.

In this society, when Black children exhibit poor reading achievement, psychologists often say it is because the children have inferior cognitive capacities. When white middle-class children have poor reading achievement, it is seldom suggested that they are unable to learn or that any deficit lies within the child. Psychologists generally say that the problem is the method of instruction or inappropriate matches between curriculum content and the child's level of development.

The Black community of educational and psychological scholars must consider seriously the need to articulate a new conceptualization of the development and behavioral styles of Black children. If we do not offer our own definitions of aptitude, intelligence, and achievement within the context of African and African-American culture, the majority of Black children will have to continue to struggle through special classes, educable mentally retarded labels, SAT and GRE scores to "make it" in this society.

The hypothesis of this book is that Black children grow up in a distinct culture. Black children therefore need an educational system that recognizes their strengths, their abilities, and their culture and that incorporates them into the learning process.

The aim of this research perspective is to describe the influence of African-American culture on child-rearing. The hypothesis is that certain characteristics, peculiar to Black culture, have their roots in West Africa and have implications for the way in which Black children learn and think.

Baratz and Baratz (1969) have focused their research upon the area of teaching Black children to read. They support the position that Black children grow up in a distinct culture that gives rise to a distinct language system in addition to distinct behavioral characteristics that are often ignored in the educative process. They charge that most educational programs are not innovative but offer smaller classes doing the same thing that large classes had been doing. These researchers say that "Black children do not need as their first priority smaller classes, intensive social programs and so forth. What they need most is an educational system that first recognizes their abilities and their culture, that draws upon these strengths and that incorporates them into the teaching process" (p. 402).

Michael Cole (1971), a researcher of cultural influences on cognition, shares the opinion that we must understand the culture of Black children if we are to gain insight into their learning styles. He suggests that more study is needed as to why problem solving and learning skills are not applied in the classroom. Even though scholars have demonstrated that Black children are using complex thinking skills on the street, the problem of transferring these skills to the classroom has not been solved. He cautions further: "But before we can do this, we must understand the nature of street and school activity. In short, we must combine ethnography and experimental psychology in the service of understanding the relation between culture and thinking" (p. 234).

The aim of this book is to review research that suggests Afro-Americans participate in a culture that has its roots in West Africa. This culture gives rise to distinctive modes of child-rearing among African-American people. As a result, Black children may have distinctive learning and expressive styles that can be observed in their play behavior. Observing child-rearing by Black parents and the play behavior of Black children may provide information about ways Black children learn. We may be able to utilize information about these learning styles to provide continuity between the behavior of parents of Black children and the behavior of teachers of Black children. We may also be able to build bridges between the natural learning styles in the family and the novel styles of learning introduced in the schools.

Attempts to understand the learning styles of Black children cannot advance without the development of an appropriate social-psychological theory of the educational process. This theory must identify the social, historical, and cultural forces that affect the development of learning styles in the Black community. This theory must also describe the psychological characteristics of Black children within the context of environmental forces that create and maintain them. It must seek to describe the cultural context out of which creative and intellectual responses occur. The thesis of this book is that psychology is social as well as personal and that we cannot separate an individual's cognitive (thinking) processes from his emotional processes.

This book should be regarded also as a statement of a problem—a working paper. It is not a finished, data-based theory. It is not a curriculum or a "how-to-teach-Black-children kit." It is a progress report. It is an attempt to share the analysis of presently existing research literature that may create a framework for such a theory. It will show data from a psychological study, the design of a proposed study, and recommendations for needed studies.

This book is multidisciplinary. It draws upon the fields of history, sociology, anthropology, psychology, music, art, philosophy, literature, theology, and education. This merging of insights from various disciplines is a necessary part of the process of honing a conceptualization of Black life. To some, the book's contents will appear fragmented. But we hope those people will pick up the fragments and begin to develop them into empirical studies. To others, the apparent diversity will converge into a perspective, an orientation, an idea, a statement—fledgling at least, thought-provoking at best.

The chapters discuss, in order, the African background, the way culture shapes cognition, culture and child-rearing, play behavior and cognitive style, the humanities and Black culture, Afro-American roots, a curriculum relevant to Afro-Americans, and implications for early childhood education.

More specifically, the first chapter looks at the distinctive features of Black life. We examine the thesis that the African heritage was not destroyed during slavery and look at the mechanisms of retention and transmission. We also examine research that has analyzed the Black community after slavery, research that suggests that Black people are sufficiently isolated in American society to preserve and transmit cultural patterns.

In chapter two, after we have shown that Black people participate in a distinctive culture, we consider evidence that culture can affect the patterns of mental abilities within ethnic groups. The concepts of cognitive style and educative style are explored and their importance in the educational performance of children is elucidated.

In chapter three, literature on five child-rearing practices is examined: 1) those practices that are an adaptation to the situation of racism and oppression that Black people have experienced in America; 2) those practices that can be characterized as family strengths, utilizing the categories set forth by Robert Hill (1972); 3) those practices that are derived from an African heritage; 4) those practices that are distinctive to Afro-American male children; and 5) those practices that are distinctive to Afro-American female children.

In chapter four we point out the value of child's play in providing information about a child's cognitive style. Play behavior is an area of psychology and early childhood education that is beginning to receive serious attention. Even though its importance is becoming increasingly apparent, research into the play behavior of Black children has been limited. Our research suggests that by obtaining information about the ways in which Black children teach themselves in early childhood and later in life, through play, we can identify and strengthen any natural learning styles they possess.

In chapter five we describe a research project that is exploring a nontraditional source of psychological data about Black culture. This project was initially funded by the A. Whitney Griswold Humanities Research Fund at Yale University. I submitted this proposal in April 1980 with the late Professor Charles Davis (professor of English and director of Afro-American Studies at Yale). It was entitled "Black Culture and Socialization." I have submitted a proposal with Professors Edmund Gordon and Vincent Franklin to the National Endowment for the Humanities for additional support.

A source of information that Black social scientists have been overlooking is the information found in the humanities. An analysis of the cultural artifacts of Afro-Americans may provide us with information about the meanings of Black culture (as it relates to socialization) from the perspective of the participants in that culture. In short, this study will provide an expanded understanding of Black culture through an analytical perspective that bridges the humanities and the social sciences.

This study is an examination of Afro-American music, art, and literature for reflections of the urban, northern, working class, contemporary Black experience (conceptualized as roughly encompassing the period between 1950 and 1980). This period was selected because previous works, notably Lawrence Levine's *Black Culture and Black Consciousness* (1977) and Thomas Webber's *Deep Like The Rivers* (1978) have analyzed music and literature that reflect the (southern) slavery and (southern/northern) post slavery/pre-World War II period.

The twentieth century has seen considerable progress in social science's understanding of the mechanisms of human growth and development. Contemporary social scientists can tell us a great deal about the interaction between human and environmental characteristics that account for behaviors. The sciences, however, have not matched the humanities in their understanding of what life means. The social sciences deal with the mechanism of human development, and the humanities deal with the meanings of human development.

The purpose of this study is to create a bridge between the social sciences and the humanities. The social sciences can be advanced by utilizing the meanings provided by the humanities. The humanities can be advanced by the influence of the structure, precision, and consensus validation of the social sciences without the loss of values derived from the subjective tradition of humanistic endeavors. As a complement, this study will reduce the unilateral focus of the social sciences on mechanisms and the unilateral focus of the humanities on meanings. Both categories would gain from such a bridge.

In this chapter the research is discussed as a fresh source for psychological hypotheses about Black culture. The methodology is described, and two examples are critiqued.

In chapter six I report my findings from my interviews with thirty Afro-American and Euro-American grandmothers who live in New Haven, Connecticut. I interviewed grandmothers to identify differences in the child-rearing values and attitudes of Afro-American women and white women of Northern European ancestry that are transmitted generationally.

During the summer of 1978 I conducted an initial investigation with open-ended interviewing of Black grandmothers in the Sea

Islands of South Carolina, reputed to be the most fertile area of the United States for identifying African retentions. These interviews laid the foundation for the development of the interview instrument utilized in this study.

The views of the grandmothers are analyzed for the information they provide in understanding socialization in Black families and behavioral styles of Black children.

Chapter seven brings together the threads that have been woven through the previous chapters. Suggestions are made for changes in existing educational policy that affects Black children. Additionally, I describe an early education model that emerges from the thesis of this book. This hypothetical model will be described in such a way that early childhood teachers will be motivated to innovate, and potential scholars will receive suggestions to direct future research efforts in this area.

One

The African Background Considered

What is Africa to me?
Copper sun or scarlet sea
Jungle star or jungle track
Strong bronzed men
Or regal Black women
From whose loins I sprang
When the birds of Eden sang.

One, three centuries removed
From the scene his fathers loved,
Spicy grove, cinnamon tree,
What is Africa to me?

—Countee Cullen*

One of the unfortunate results of the American slavery experience was the de-Africanization experience that converted the African into a Negro. The newly arrived Africans were prohibited from using their native language and were forced to adopt the English language along with its view of the universe. They were forced to learn words and systems of thought that defined their color as evil and their culture as heathen and savage. They were forced to accept new names. No longer were they Yorubas, Ashantis or Akans. Now they were coloreds, niggers, or Negroes. One of the unanswered questions of history is how complete the de-Africanization process was. Should we conceptualize the African as an eager student of American behaviors and values? Or should we conceive of him as a shrewd survivor, who absorbed what was necessary while he re-

---

*From "Heritage" from *On These I Stand* by Countee Cullen. Copyright 1925 by Harper & Row, Publishers, renewed 1953 by Ida M. Cullen. Reprinted by permission of the publisher. (First stanza.)

sisted complete immersion in American culture? Another possibility is that African culture may have survived and may have been transmitted without conscious effort on the part of African-American people. The aspects of African culture that survived may have been so subtle and so ingrained in Black behavior patterns that they are not thought of as Africanisms. They may simply be thought of as "the way" that Black people cook, walk, dance, dress, and talk.

It is not the purpose of this chapter to suggest that all aspects of Black behavior can be traced to African influences. Clearly, an interaction has taken place between the African heritage and the American experience. However, I believe the American experience of Black people has been emphasized in any analysis of Black behavior rather than the interaction between the two cultures.

Developing a socio-psychological theory of the development of Black children is a very difficult task. Therefore, every avenue of investigation must be explored. This chapter does not present *proof* beyond doubt that African culture survived slavery. But it does present evidence to persuade the reader that the theory is a possibility worthy of further investigation.

As we consider the issue of whether a distinct culture is shared by Black people in this country, we need to begin by reviewing the question of whether the African heritage was destroyed during slavery.

Orlando Patterson (1972, pp. 29–31) has suggested three ways of viewing Black history. The first is the *catastrophic* view, which maintains that Black history in the New World is a long list of disasters and horrors caused by white oppression. This point of view is reflected in the writings of E. Franklin Frazier, Malcolm X, and Nathan Hare. Their perspective may have laid the foundation for the compensatory education movement. In other words, if sociological scholars demonstrated that the Black community had been devastated by the slavery and post-slavery experience, extra compensation should restore and rebuild the Black family and its community. The problem with this point of view is that it overlooks any adaptive mechanisms that Black people may have developed to facilitate their survival. Also, the danger exists of adopting the Anglo-Saxon family as the model that Black families should emulate. The contemporary upheavals between white parents and their children and white women and men are indications that this is not a desirable goal.

The second point of view is *contributionism.* This view is concerned with the Black man's contributions to "civilization." The approach traditionally discussed the contribution to American civilization. But most people play down the American contribution as irrelevant because America is regarded as a sinking ship. Instead, they head for the civilization "big time"—Carthage and Egypt and the "great" civilizations of North Africa and the Near East. According to Patterson (1972), "The overwhelming drift of Black historical consciousness today is toward the grand version of contributionism" (p. 29).

The third perspective is called *survivalist*. This view does not deny the horrors of slavery, but it sees the Black man as having triumphed in maintaining his African roots in spite of a destructive and hostile environment. The major proponent of this view was a white American anthropologist, Melville Herskovits.

We will consider the survivalist perspective in the present discussion. If we are to establish the fact that Black people have a distinctive culture, we must look at whether the African heritage was destroyed during slavery, and if it was transmitted, what the mechanisms of retention and transmission were.

When Herskovits (1958) did his work in the 1930s, it was not well received either by the Black or by the white communities. He wrote that "scholars did not search for Africanisms in the behavior of Black people because the African experience was defined as disgraceful" (p. 27). This society had perpetuated the myth that Africans had no culture or civilization and that they swung through trees and ate each other. They taught Black Americans that Blacks had attained the highest level of culture by having been brought to America and having been civilized by the white man. Illustrating this point of view, N. S. Shaler (1890) suggested in an article that a worthwhile research question might be to measure the size of the brain of a native African and compare it to the size of the brain of a Black American to determine whether the Black American's brain had grown from his association with the white man (p. 29).

Confronted with this kind of prejudice, Black people were not interested in Africa and preferred not to be reminded of their African heritage.

Herskovits (1939) saw far-reaching educational implications in his work:

When, for instance, one sees vast programs of Negro education undertaken without the slightest consideration being given to even the possibility of some retention of African thought and speech that might influence the Negroes' reception of the instruction thus offered, one cannot but ask how we hope to reach the desired objectives. We are amazed when we are confronted with psychological studies of race relations made in utter ignorance of characteristic African patterns of motivation and behavior, or with sociological analyses of Negro family life which make not the slightest attempt to take into account even the chance that the phenomena being studied might in some way have been influenced by the carry-over of certain African traditions (p. 93).

Ulf Hannerz (1974) suggests that Black American ways of life were influenced throughout the American experience by three kinds of forces: 1) the weight of Black community tradition, 2) the pressure to conform to mainstream American culture, and 3) the particular structural conditions deriving from being placed quite consistently at the bottom of American society.

Hannerz notes that the tools of anthropology may be most useful in analyzing the culture of Afro-American people. Sociologists, he says, tend to view the dominant society as given and to define other groups as deviant depending upon the extent to which they conform to the structure of that society. Anthropologists, on the other hand, have relativist and comparativist traditions and expect to find cultural differences among groups and to explain them as such rather than as deviance. He observes further that some anthropologists are describing an Afro-American continuum which suggests continuities between Black people in the Caribbean, Latin America, North America, and the Canadian seaboard. He too suggests more research into the continuous interplay between Black cultural tradition and American social structure. He notes correctly that Black American tradition is no longer only a matter of an African heritage, but is also the shared experience of slavery and southern rural poverty, as well as traditions already evolving in the urban setting. Hannerz concludes his analysis as follows:

The synthesis must also include a third element besides Black cultural tradition and socioeconomic pressures: inputs of mainstream culture. The autonomous Black culture is an elusive entity. In one context, it may come clearly to the fore; in the next, one wonders if one sees anything that other Americans would not do. . . . One needs a conceptual framework where the possibility is recognized that an individual can have more than one culture in his repertoire, that he can switch between these cultures quickly and that he can drift between them over a longer period. I myself tried to develop a concept of biculturalism as a tool for understanding the ghetto cultural situation (p. 153).

African-Americans Resisted Slavery

In determining whether Africanisms were retained, we must consider whether Blacks accepted slavery. We must concede at the outset that the surface has only been scratched in investigating the reaction of Black people to slavery. We need an extensive investigation of the acculturative process and the reaction of Black people to enslavement and slave status. The traditional interpretation of Black history has emphasized the acquiescence of Blacks to slavery. Herskovits (1958) points out behaviors of the slaves that can be interpreted as covert mechanisms of resistance to slavery. Recognizing this resistance is important because, as Herskovits maintains, slaves who acquiesced in their status would be more prone to accept the culture of their masters than those who rebelled. Similarly, if they were reluctant to accept slave status, they would have struggled harder to retain what they could of their African culture and heritage.

One needs only to check the record of the numerous slave revolts to concur that the slaves were at least restless (p. 86). However, open revolt was not the only way in which Blacks protested slavery. Usually they were not able to organize protests among themselves; therefore individuals protested as best they could. One of the most common methods of protesting was slowing down work, purposely mutilating crops, and misusing implements furnished by the slave-owner. Some slaveowners attributed such transgressions to the innate shiftlessness and irresponsibility of Blacks. However, the literature abounds with examples of the extent to which Blacks worked well without supervision, cultivated plots of ground after hours, demonstrated competence in skilled trades as they worked to purchase their freedom, or became free, self-employed workers (p. 99).

Suicide, infanticide, and poisoning can be interpreted also as expressions of resistance to slave status. Suicide was reported to have been so pervasive that slaveowners denied Christian burial rites to offenders and branded them as criminals (p. 102). The mortality rate of newborn Black infants was so high in some areas that some slaveowners made it the responsibility of the overseer to assure the survival of babies. However, some scholars suggest that neither ignorance nor indifference of the slave women to their offspring accounted for the number of children who died soon after being born; rather, their deaths may have been attributed to a desire not to bring children into the world to live under slavery (p. 103). Nat Turner's African-born mother (he was the leader of a major slave revolt) had to be tied at Nat's birth to be prevented from murdering him (p. 102).

Running away was also quite pervasive, and this can be interpreted as another form of protest. Some southern writers described it as a disease called "monomania," to which the Black race is peculiarly susceptible. Olmsted (1860) characterizes this explanation as "making the common mistake of attributing to blood that which is more rationally to be traced to condition" (p. 228). Even though risks were great and punishments severe, thousands of men and women took flight.

Herskovits looks at the acculturative process for evidence of opportunities for slaves to have preserved African culture. As with the other points raised, he admits that the data are scanty and scattered and that intensive research will be needed before any conclusions can be drawn. However, he pulls together evidence in the literature worth considering. When African slaves arrived at the plantation, they were placed in the charge of trusted slaves for the "seasoning" process. The customary assumption is that the slave teachers had such an abhorrence for "savage" ways that there was no opportunity for any interchange that could have reinforced Africanisms present in the teachers or the newcomers. Even though this assumption is made, the relationship between Africans and their teachers has not been systematically studied. The only evidence that has been explored is the customary plantation routine for orienting newcomers. Herskovits postulated that once rapport was established and language barriers transcended, the African may have met a real need in the life of the Black born in slavery to fill in gaps in the world-view and religious conceptualizations that were left purposely by slaveowners. The African having come from a sophisticated culture was in a position to retransmit and reinforce customs already being practiced on a more humble level. At a minimum, this constant incorporation of African Blacks may have retarded a too rapid or too complete adoption of white values (p. 131).

West Africa is the Source of African-American Africanisms

Herskovits narrows the search for Africanisms to West Africa. He reviews the evidence suggesting that Black people on this continent came primarily from that area. Analysis of the manifests of slaving ships at the ports of Maryland, Virginia, South Carolina, and Georgia show the numbers of slaves carried by each vessel and the ports from which this human cargo was obtained. These data show, as Herskovits states, that the Negroes brought to America were "in the main of West African descent. For the most part, they were brought or captured along the West Coast, and the Guinea Negroes were by far the most numerous, constituting well over fifty per cent of the total importation" (p. 133).

He states further that even if Blacks were brought later from other areas, the new arrivals would be acculturated into the behavior styles of the Blacks already here (p. 52).

African retentions are more evident in the Black communities of Dutch Guiana, Jamaica, Haiti, Brazil, and Cuba. Intensive study of their place names, religious rites, names of gods, and customs of a social and political nature shows that they can be traced to West Africa (Herskovits 1936, p. 22).

In looking for retentions among Blacks in the United States, Herskovits (1951) states that it will be most fruitful to study those who are lower-class because those who are in the more privileged sectors of the society have more access to the cultural resources of the dominant group, and the retentions are less pure. In the United States, in addition to differences made by socio-economic status, are geographical differences. Fertile areas for observing Africanisms in the United States are in the coastal (Sea Islands) areas of South Carolina and Georgia. However, most retentions in the United States are not evident in pure form but are reinterpreted because of the extent of acculturation of Blacks to this society. So the student of retentions must raise his research efforts from the elementary level of description and comparison to the more sophisticated analysis of process (pp. 123–47).

I will not attempt in this limited space to explore all of the analysis offered by Herskovits (1958). But it may be instructive to review a list of aspects of Black culture that reflect Africanisms:

• Funerals

• Magical practices

• Folklore (Uncle Remus stories are similar to the sacred myths of Africa.)

• Dance

• Song

• Motor Habits (walking, speaking, laughing, sitting, postures, burden carrying, dancing, singing, hoeing, and movements made in various agricultural and industrial activities)

• Ways of dressing hair (wrapping, braiding, cornrowing)

• Wearing of headkerchiefs, scarves (Women of the African diaspora tend to wear hair coverings more than European women. In the United States Black women wear scarves; in the Caribbean they wear bandannas, and in Africa they wear *gélés*.)

• Etiquette
   a. During slavery when Black people were denied titles such as Mister or Mistress, they substituted other titles of respect. Therefore, older people were called "Uncle" or "Aunt" or "Brother Jones" or "Sister Jones."

   In African societies the ancestors are the most respected strata of the family. The elderly are the closest to the ancestors;

therefore they are accorded a great deal of respect. Consequently, Black people of the diaspora have been observed to accord great respect to the elderly.

b. Black culture encouraged turning the head when laughing, placing the hand over the mouth, or in speaking to elders or other respected persons averting the eyes and perhaps the face. Some people thought that when Black children turned their heads, it was a sign of inattention, but in light of their West African roots, it is interpreted to be a mark of respect.

- Concept of time

Black people think in terms of approximations of time rather than punctuality. An "in-house" expression is "C.P.T."—meaning "Colored People's Time"! When a meeting is scheduled, one Black person might ask another whether they mean Eastern Standard Time or Colored People's Time. Meetings that begin on C.P. Time usually begin about twenty minutes after the appointed time.

I was amazed when traveling to West Africa and Jamaica to find a similar joke in those places about "African time" and "Jamaican time." Meetings that began on Jamaican time often began as much as ninety minutes after the appointed time!

John Mbiti (1970) has analyzed the African conception of time within the context of African religious and philosophical systems.

- Cooperation and sharing (Black people have expressed an orientation toward collective responsibility and interdependence.)

- Child-rearing practices (Corporal punishment [whipping] is used in disciplining children. The most common instrument is the "switch" [a long, thin twig from a tree that is stripped of its leaves].)

- Adoption of Children (Black people exhibit a strong orientation toward adopting children. Robert Hill (1972) has pointed out that Black people don't go to adoption agencies to adopt children; their applications would be rejected. However, an informal system of adoption operates, wherein usually older women will care for children when their families need assistance.)

- Myths about abnormal births in the folklore of Africa and the United States have been found to be similar.

- Child-naming practices

- Audience and performer styles (A highly emotional interaction exists between Black performers and audiences, with a great deal of call and response. Usually the better known and respected a performer, the more vociferous the response. The performer will be encouraged by shouts of "Amen!" "Right-on!" "Get-down!" "Get-off!" "Take your time!" "Make it plain!" and so forth, depending upon whether it is a sacred or secular setting. In contrast, European-oriented audiences will indicate attention by silence, eye-contact, and laughter when appropriate (Roger Abrahams 1970).

- Religious and spiritual expressive styles are highly emotional overtones to worship.

- Conception of the devil

Slavery Reexamined

Traditional studies of slavery have emphasized the institution of slavery rather than the culture of the slaves. V. P. Franklin (1974) points out that most historians have ignored the writing of slaves and ex-slaves and have devoted their attention to the documents of Southern planters. He points out further that a distinctive slave culture existed that had a profound effect on personality development and enabled Blacks to survive the cruelties of American slavery. Franklin says that most analyses of slave personality proceed from the perspective of role theory in which "emphasis was placed on the institution of slavery and its probable influence upon the individual slave" (p. 61). The approach he suggests would shift the emphasis to the individual slave, his family, and his culture:

Shifting to an emphasis on Black culture and its effect on slave personality is extremely important in that it allows us to reinterpret the significance of Black culture in the lives of slaves and freedmen. Previous interpretations of slave culture have considered it merely the way the slaves passed their spare time (p. 60).

John Blassingame (1972) writes that slaves had a culture with which they identified as a group:

The most important aspect of this group identification was that the slaves were not solely dependent on the white man's cultural frames of reference for their ideals and values. As long as the plantation Black had cultural norms and ideals, ways of verbalizing aggression, and roles in his life largely free from his master's control, he would preserve some personal autonomy, and resist infantilization, total identification with planters, and internalization of unflattering stereotypes calling for abject servility (p. 41).

Blassingame and Franklin clearly point out the need for a study of slavery that assumes the cultural integrity of the slave.

The presented evidence suggests that the culture of Black people neither began nor ended with the experience of slavery. Even though the acculturation process and the slavery experience may have altered the African culture that was transmitted, enough mechanisms of retention and transmission existed for survivals to have been possible.

Transmission of Black Culture After Slavery

We will now consider whether and in what manner these distinctive elements of culture could have been retained and transmitted since slavery.

Considerable evidence supports the view that Black people have been so isolated in this society that they have been able to participate in a distinctive culture. This isolation is particularly true of the poor. Charles Valentine (1968) has identified three general positions that have characterized the poor:

1. a self-perpetuating subsociety with a deficient unhealthy subculture;
2. a subculture that is oppressed from the outside by the larger society with a culture that is exposed and exploited;
3. a variable subsociety with many adaptive subcultures.

The first position (that the poor are deficient) is the orientation of academic poverty experts. The third position, which is Valentine's (that the poor live in a subsociety consisting of a number of subcultures that are adaptive rather than deficient), is the view that will be considered here (p. 144).

Robin Williams (1964) studied the present-day Black community. His research supports the findings that Black people are sufficiently isolated in this society to preserve and transmit cultural patterns:

Blacks tend to belong to all-Negro churches, voluntary organizations, information groups, and to experience the bulk of their social interaction with other local Negroes, despite possible inter-racial contacts in their work, school and shopping life (p. 236).

The literature substantiates that membership in the Black culture has an effect on a wide range of behavior. For example, Henderson (1967) presents data to show that Black youth tend to perform very much alike on such measures of social performance as education achievement, law-violating behavior, aspirations, and perceptions of life chances. Even when they compared Black youth from poverty and nonpoverty families, broken homes, and intact homes, the trend among Blacks persisted when compared to whites. He concluded that the most valid variable was participating in the Black cultural system (p. 138).

Johnson and Sanday (1971) found other themes they felt characterize Blacks, for example that Black people, unlike white people, have a central theme of survival. The necessity they have faced to make continual adaptations to the American social order has destroyed for them an orientation to opportunity* and a trust in other people (p. 137).

Another of Johnson's and Sanday's defining characteristics separating Black and white people is the differential access each group has to the resources of society. The white cultural group, which has free access, has created two social systems or structural arrangements of people in the American society—one Black and one white. This is exemplified by a racially segregated school system, Blacks living on a subsistence and whites living in a monetary economy, and several systems of law enforcement (p. 139).

Henderson (1967) suggests further that several forces keep the cultural system intact—racial, mental, physical, and social isolation. The system is set up so that contact between the races is minimal. This system is maintained by the external design of the system and also by internal factors operating within the Black community to maintain cohesiveness (p. 138).

It is therefore clearly possible that Black culture could have been transmitted across generations. Black people live, study, work, and socialize together because of the way in which housing, school, employment opportunities, and social stratification have been designed by "the powers that be." But it is also true that Black people enjoy being together and that they feel more comfortable when they can experience the beauty and the joy of Blackness.

---

*It is not clear how Johnson and Sanday are conceptualizing "an orientation to opportunity." However, Afro-Americans have displayed a remarkable resiliency in striving to achieve in the face of overwhelming odds. The orientation to opportunity is clearly present among Afro-American people although its expression may occur through nontraditional mechanisms.

Two

How Culture
Shapes Cognition

The Negro is a sort of seventh son, born with a veil, and gifted with second-sight in this American world—a world which yields him no true self-conciousness, but only lets him see himself through the revelation of the other world. . . . One ever feels his two-ness—an American, a Negro; two souls, two thoughts, two unreconciled strivings; two warring ideals in one dark body, whose dogged strength alone keeps it from being torn asunder.

—W. E. B. DuBois

W. E. B. DuBois described the Black person in America as possessing two "warring souls." On the one hand, Black people are products of their Afro-American heritage and culture. On the other hand, they are shaped by the demands of Anglo-American culture.

In the previous chapter, evidence suggests that Black people participate in a distinctive culture. We will now consider the body of literature that maintains one's culture affects one's cognitive processes. The end-point of this analysis is that Black people participate in a coherent culture that shapes their cognitive development and affects the way they approach academic tasks and the way they behave in traditional academic settings.

Biology and Culture

The work of Jean Piaget is being considered and accepted by American psychologists. He gives attention to maturational and biological factors in the development of cognition. However, Ward (1973, p. 2) raises the question "How much of the variance among peoples is attributable to culture and how much to maturational and other factors? The present state of the art does not allow us to make a definitive statement." Piaget (1966, pp. 3–13) himself admits the problem:

The kind of psychology we develop in our social environments remains con-jectural as long as comparative, extensive and systematic research is not available; a great effort is still to be made in this direction. . . . Only such studies allow us to separate the effects of biological and mental factors from those of social and cultural influences on the formation and socialization of individuals.

Ward states further the consensus of some scholars:

[They] argue that language and culture virtually program the mind so that the individual as a learner is both bounded and shaped according to the world-and-life view and the mental-process styles of his culture. Others, such as Piaget and Chomsky, give a much larger place to constants in language, maturation, mental operations and universal interactions (such as coopera-tions, oppositions, exchanges) and a much smaller place to transmissions which vary from culture to culture (p. 2).

Even though the biological aspects of cognition that humans uni-versally share have received the most attention, scholars are begin-ning to look at deviations from the norms and the extent to which culture may account for differences among groups. Flavell (1963, p.

Can we build a bridge between the natural learning styles utilized in the fam-ily and the novel style of learning introduced in the school?

20) has noted that "Piaget has . . . for a long time freely conceded that not all 'normal' adults, even within one culture, end up at a common generic level. Adults will show adult thought only in those content areas in which they have been socialized."

This new direction of investigation suggests that cognition is social as well as biological. It looks at the relationship between one's culture and the kinds of cognitive skills one develops. Michael Cole (1971, p. 20), a noted researcher in this area, looks at cognition in conjunction with the other activities of life. He believes that "the study of cognitive processes cannot ignore content, particularly the basic categories of experience that are relevant to the processes under scrutiny. Finally ethnographic analysis sets a kind of endpoint of any analysis of cognition; it provides a picture of the intelligent, adaptive behaviors that people engage in every day."

Most of the work that has been done on comparative cognition has looked at thinking in different cultures that are geographically separated. Much of that research has centered around African societies. (Witkin 1967, Textor 1967, Hovey 1971).

Ward (1973, p. 4) suggests that this new interest in cross-cultural educational research has created a new awareness among educators of the tools of anthropology. Cross-cultural instructional issues have been placed into anthropological perspective.

He describes the process for the adaptation of instructional materials to a different culture:

Level 1: Translation (language)
Level 2: Adjusting the vocabulary (to make the reading level of the adapted material match the level of the original)
Level 3: Changing the illustrations to refer to local experiences
Level 4: Restructuring the instructional procedures implied and/or specified to accommodate pedagogical expectations of the learners
Level 5: Recasting the content to reflect local world-and-life views
Level 6: Accommodating the learning styles ("cognitive styles") of the learners

The problems associated with levels one through three are relatively easy to understand and address. However, the problems associated with levels five and six are more difficult because of limited understanding of the learner's world-and-life view, of the concept of cognitive style, and the relationship between the two.

Witkin (1967, p. 234) defines cognitive style as "the characteristic self-consistent modes of functioning found pervasively throughout an individual's cognitive activities" (perceptual and intellectual).

In Africa I had an opportunity to talk with Dr. Romanus Ohuche of the University of Sierra Leone and other African psychologists who are applying the work of Jean Piaget and studying concept development among African children. These psychologists believe that Piagetian theory and the growing body of knowledge related to it, at present, provide a useful framework within which to undertake empirical research and to apply research findings to curriculum design. One of the reasons they look favorably upon Piaget's work is that the major aspects of his theory can be applied to all human societies and groups, and differences in performance can be accounted for without imputing inferiority or deficiency.

Piaget (1966) distinguishes four factors that influence the development of cognitive functions:

1. biological factors, which account for the invariant sequence of stages
2. equilibration factors, which arise through interaction with the environment and determine the development of mental operations
3. general socialization factors or social interactions between individuals, which are identical for all societies
4. social factors, which differ from one society to another, and include particularly factors of educational and cultural transmission.

Certain aspects of Black Culture reflect Africanisms.

These factors do not operate independently, but the second and fourth do vary from one society to another, and may be used as a basis for investigating differences in performance in cultural subgroups.

Even though Piaget's work has potential for cross-cultural research, certain methodological defects will have to be corrected. Raphael Nyiti (1976, p. 1122) pointed out three such problems in the application of Piaget's clinical method to research of mastery of conservation among children of Tanzania:

1. linguistic and cultural barriers between the subject and the investigator
2. the tendency to treat Piaget's conservation tasks as performance tests
3. the determination of subject's ages from estimates or unreliable sources

At a conference held in Sierra Leone, West Africa, by UNICEF in 1974 to study the development of mathematical and scientific skills by African children, a group of African scholars outlined areas of Piaget's work that need further investigation to describe concept development among African children:

• the opportunities given for play and manipulative activities among children and the relationship of such activities to concept development
• appropriate interview procedures used to ascertain the characteristics of African children's thinking
• the extent to which the mother tongue affects the learning of concepts in a new language
• the effect of bilingualism and multilingualism on the development of concepts (This was particularly interesting to me because most of the children I encountered in Africa spoke from three to seven languages.)
• in the context of environmental circumstances, to what extent various wasting diseases and deficiency diseases affect intellectual growth
• against the different social and cultural backgrounds, the extent to which African cosmology influences the development of concepts (African scholars have hypothesized that the rituals and magico-religious beliefs may affect the development of concepts in African children.)
• the games, riddles, and proverbs found among African groups and their effect on concept development

- the concept of "intelligence" or "cleverness" as it is understood among African groups
- parental attitudes toward schooling and the influence these exert upon concept development (Available evidence suggests that parental attitudes seem to be more important than family income in determining the performance of children.)
- the development of relevant social concepts, such as kinship, chieftaincy, presidency, and the like
- the precocity of African babies and the extent to which it is maintained over a period of time

Social Class and Ethnicity

An issue that has received considerable attention in studies of culture and cognition is the relative influence of social class and ethnicity. The consensus seems to be that social class and ethnicity interact in the shaping of human behavior, but this interaction is a complex process (Havighurst 1976, p. 62).

Havighurst (p. 56) writes that within a complex society, social classes and ethnic groups are the two major ecological structures that produce diversity in human life style and development. Each

Ethnic groups are people who have a common history and generally share a language, a religion, or a racial identity. Each ethnic group forms a subculture with its own attitudes and behaviors.

social class system consists of groups of people who each have a set of behaviors and attitudes that define it and separate it from the other social classes. Similarly, the system of ethnic groups consists of groups of people who each have a common history and generally share a language, a religion, or a racial identity. Each ethnic group forms a subculture with its own attitudes and behaviors.

Havighurst (p. 57) states further that cultural patterns are transmitted (socialization occurs) within social class and ethnic groups through the same mechanisms: family, peer group, common literature, formal associations, in-group marriage, and residential segregation. "Thus in a consideration of social class as an ecological factor or set of forces in human development and behavior, ethnicity always stands at the side of the stage, ready to explain some of the phenomena which cannot be understood by social class considerations alone."

This issue becomes increasingly complex as one attempts to sort out the influence of Black ethnicity and social class. Havighurst (p. 62) sets forth a model to show the relative strength of social class and ethnicity among ethnic groups in the USA. He suggests that "ethnicity outweighs social class in the upper-middle class of European Jewish Americans and of Japanese and Chinese Americans, while social class outweighs ethnicity in the upper-middle-class Blacks, South and East European ethnics, and Americans of Spanish origins." He suggests further that middle-class values enhance rather than compete with the values of European whites, Jew, Chinese, and Japanese. However, in his analysis Black and Spanish ethnicity do not seem to correlate well with upper-middle-class life style. Therefore, ethnicity has less influence on the behavior of middle-class Blacks and Americans of Spanish origin. On the other hand, the influence of ethnicity is stronger than social class influences among the lower classes of those groups.

I am not totally convinced by the foregoing analysis. First of all, present measures of social class may not be relevant for Black people. Many families are classified as middle-class on the basis of the income and occupation of the parents in the nuclear family. However, in the present discussion we are concerned with the belief systems and values that are transmitted through socialization. Therefore, the nuclear family is a part of a network through which it is connected to the culture of the Black community. Through this network the child is the recipient of values from both the lower and middle social classes. Even though the parents in the nuclear family may be classified as middle-class in terms of their adult-achieved status, they may well have received their socialization in families that would be classified as lower-class. Therefore, aspects of the interaction of ethnicity and lower-class values would be inadvertently present in their child-rearing. Also, not to be overlooked is that Black children are socialized by their grandparents and other kin and para-kinship persons in the community. It would be difficult to identify a child in the Black community who is socialized in middle-class values in an isolated fashion. It may be necessary to create a new paradigm to interpret social class influences among Black people. It may be useful to analyze the occupation, income, and values of several generations in order to construct a relevant picture of the social network in which present child-rearing occurs.

S. B. Sarason (1973, p. 965) postulates that psychologists and educators must consider attitudes that are shaped by one's ethnic culture. He describes "Jewishness" and "Blackishness" as descriptors for people who have Jewish and Afro-American ethnicity. People who are socialized in those cultures are imbued with attitudes and characteristics that are rooted in history. These characteristics, he indicates, are "a kind of 'second nature', learned, absorbed, and inculcated with all the force, subtleness, and efficiency of the processes of cultural transmission." To understand the tenacity of these characteristics requires a time perspective of centuries. Therefore, it would require long periods of time to dilute or extinguish them. Sarason states further that "it is impossible to understand and evaluate intellectual performance of groups without taking account of each group's attitudes toward such activity. This is an obvious point to anyone who has engaged in clinical work and it has received substantial support in the research literature, for example, the test anxiety literature. It is no less valid a point when one deals with the intellectual performance of historically rooted groups and their historically rooted attitudes" (p. 965). He points out that the achievement of females may be shaped by their attitudes toward certain activities as well. Finally, he predicts that this central psychological core of historically rooted groups cannot change in a lifetime.

Stodolsky and Lesser (1967, p. 546) discuss the orientation of social science research and the formulation of social policy. They describe the orientation of "disadvantaged" advocates as taking the position that lower-class families should be provided with what a middle-class family has—better jobs, education, and housing. This will produce levels of mental ability in lower-class children that resemble that of middle-class children. However, they raise the question raised in this chapter, of what happens to this concept when the issue of ethnicity is introduced. Their research suggests that ethnic groups differ in their patterns of ability no matter what the social-class level is within the ethnic group. The educational problem presented by these findings becomes a matter of providing educational resources to develop maximally the abilities of all ethnic groups even at the expense of magnifying the differences between the groups. The orientation of most education research is to minimize, decrease, or ignore differences between ethnic groups so that education can proceed more easily and economically.

Stodolsky and Lesser state the aims of their research as follows:

Our goal was to examine the patterns among various mental abilities in six- and seven-year-old children from different social class and ethnic backgrounds. We accepted the definition of intelligence which postulates diverse mental abilities and proposes that intelligent behavior can be manifested in a variety of forms, with each individual displaying certain areas of intellectual strength and other forms of intellectual weakness. A basic premise of this study is that social-class and ethnic influences differ not only in degree but in kind, with the consequence that different kinds of intellectual skills are fostered or hindered in different environments (p. 569).

They studied Chinese, Jewish, Black, and Puerto Rican children. Each ethnic group was divided into middle- and lower-class, as well as male and female. They studied four mental abilities: verbal ability, reasoning, number facility, and space conceptualization. The findings of the study suggest that distinctive differences exist among the ethnic groups. The order of performance for the various ethnic groups was as follows:

Afro-Americans: verbal ability, reasoning, space conceptualization, number ability

Chinese: space conceptualization, number ability, reasoning, verbal

Jewish: verbal, number ability, reasoning, space conceptualization

Puerto Rican: space conceptualization, number ability, reasoning, verbal

Each group was markedly different both in the *level* of each mental ability and in the *pattern* of these abilities. The most interesting finding of the study was that social class variation within the ethnic group does not alter the basic organization or pattern of mental abilities peculiar to that group. This finding was unexpected because social-class influences have been described as superseding ethnic-group influences "for such diverse phenomena as child-rearing practices, educational and occupational aspirations, achievement motivation, and anomie [normlessness]. . . ." (p. 570). Actually, the assumption that ethnic groups have more in common because of social class than greater differences due to ethnicity has been the rationale behind diverse groups being grouped together as "disadvantaged" and treated as a unit. It is instructive to note that the differences in mental abilities between lower-class and middle-class children were greater in the Black group than in the other groups. However, the middle-class children across the groups resembled each other more than the lower-class children across the groups. Therefore, social class is a factor; but ethnicity emerged as the primary factor (p. 571).

Three questions have been raised regarding this research that can direct future efforts.

1. To what extent are mental-ability patterns predictors of school achievement? Is there *one* pattern of mental ability that results in overall superior school performance, or are different patterns associated with superior school performance in *different subject matter areas*? If optimal patterns are identified, should the child's abilities be reinforced so that these patterns are produced, or should the educational program be adjusted to fit the strengths and weaknesses of the child (p. 578)?

2. How stable are the patterns of abilities over time? Do the rates for learning eventually level off, or do they represent stable cognitive organizations? What role does the school experience play in modifying distinctive ethnic-group patterns (p. 579)?

3. How can instructional strategies be matched to the child's patterns of mental abilities (p. 580)?

This research highlights a major problem in social policy that addresses the learning problems of ethnic groups in general and the lower classes within those groups in particular. Even though it is a worthwhile effort to elevate the standard of living and social-class position of lower-class children, that may not be the "end-all" that has been assumed. These children would still retain the distinctive mental-ability pattern associated with their ethnic group. So the question becomes one of how we can make maximum use of these distinctive patterns of ability. The authors suggest that the line of future investigation should focus on matching instructional strategies to the patterns of mental ability (pp. 584–85).

Cognitive Style

Rosalie Cohen (1969) has identified two styles of learning. One is called the analytical style and the other is the relational style. These styles refer to differences in the methods of selecting and classifying information. She suggests that some individuals are "splitters" and others are "lumpers." Kagan, Moss, and Siegal (1963) write:

Cognitive style *refers to the process of utilizing "logical skills."*

"Lumpers" are individuals who think attributes of a stimulus have significance in themselves; "splitters" think they have significance only in reference to some total context.

Asa Hilliard (1976) has compiled a summary of the characteristics of two of the styles identified by Cohen (see Table 1).

Two processes are measured by standardized tests and rewarded in the school. One process refers to the method of selecting and organizing information. The other process is the growth of information. Cognitive style refers to the process of utilizing "logical" skills.

The school requires one specific approach to cognitive organization—analytic (Cohen 1969, p. 829). Pupils who have not developed these skills and those who function with a different cognitive style will not only be poor achievers early in school, but they will also become worse as they move to higher grade levels.

Table 2, developed by Cohen (p. 839), summarizes the predicted achievement of students who function with high or low information in the analytic or relational mode.

Table 1

Analytical and Relational Cognitive Styles
(Compiled from Rosalee Cohen. In Hilliard 1976, pp. 36–40.)

Analytical Style

Stimulus centered.
Parts-specific.
Finds nonobvious attributes.
Abstracts common or generalizable principle of a stimulus.
Notices formal properties of a stimulus that have relatively stable and long-lasting meanings.
Ignores the idiosyncratic.
Extracts from embedded context.
Names extracted properties and gives them meaning in themselves.
Relationships tend to be linear.
Relationships that are noticed tend to be static and descriptive rather than functional or inferential.
Relationships seldom involve process or motivation as a basis for relations.
Perception of conceptual distance between observers and observed.
An objective attitude—a belief that everything takes place "out there" in the stimulus.
Stimulus viewed as formal, long lasting, and relatively constant; therefore opportunity exists to study it in detail.
Long attention span.
Long concentration span.
Greater perceptual vigilance.
A reflective attitude and relatively sedentary nature.
Language style is standard English of controlled elaboration.
Language depends upon relatively long-lasting and stable meanings of words.
Language depends upon formal and stable rules of organization.
Communications are intended to be understood in themselves, i.e., without dependence upon nonverbal cues or idiosyncratic context.
"Parts of speech" can readily be seen in nonsense sentences.
Analytic speech characterized by "hesitation phenomena": pauses for verbal planning by controlled vocal modulation and revision of sentence organization to convey specific meaning, since words have formal meanings.
Sometimes view of self expressed as an aspect of roles, such as function to be performed.
View of self tends to be in terms of status role.

Relational Style

Self-centered.
Global.
Fine descriptive characteristics.
Identifies the unique.
Ignores commonalities.
Embedded for meaning.
Relevant concepts must have special or personal relevance to observer.
Meanings are unique, depending upon immediate context.
Generalizations and linear notions are generally unused and devalued.
Parts of the stimulus and its nonobvious attributes are not given names and appear to have no meaning in themselves.

33

Table 1 (Continued)

Relationships tend to be functional and inferential.

Since emphasis is placed on the unique and the specific, the global, and the discrete, on notions of difference rather than on variation or common things, the search for mechanism to form abstract generalizations is not stimulated.

Responses tend to be affective.

Perceived conceptual distance between the observer and the observed is narrow.

The field is perceived as responding to the person.

The field may have a life of its own.

Personification of the inanimate.

Distractible.

Emotional.

Over-involved in all activities.

Easily angered by minor frustrations.

Immediacy of response.

Short attention span.

Short concentration span.

Gestalt learners.

Descriptive abstraction for word selection.

Words must be embedded in specific time-bound context for meaning.

Few synonyms in language.

Language dependent upon unique context and upon many interactional characteristics of the communicants on time and place, on inflection, muscular movements, and other nonverbal cues.

Fluent spoken language.

Strong, colorful expressions.

Wide range of meaningful vocal intonation and inflection.

Condensed conditions, sensitivity to hardly perceptible variations of mood and tone in other individuals and in their surroundings.

Poor response to timed, scheduled, preplanned activities that interfere with immediacy of response.

Tends to ignore structure.

Self-descriptions tend to point to essence.

Table 2

Orientation to school requirements by skill-information combinations

Skill-information combinations	Orientation to school requirements
High analytic skills, high information	High achievement, high I.Q.*, high success in school
High analytic skills, low information	High achievement, average I.Q.*, anxiety (overachievers)
High relational skills, high information	Low achievement, high I.Q.*, behavior problems (underachievers)
High relational skills, low information	Low achievement, low I.Q.*, complete inability to relate to the school, withdrawal and drop-out

*Tested I.Q.
Cohen 1969, p. 837

The school requires one specific approach to cognitive organization—analytic.

Not only does the school reward the development of the analytic style of processing information, but its overall ideology and environment reinforces behaviors associated with that style. "Aspects of analytic style can be found in the requirements that the pupil learn to sit increasingly long periods of time, to concentrate alone on impersonal learning stimuli, and to observe and value organized time-allotment schedules" (p. 830).

The differences between children who function with relational and analytic styles is so great that a child whose cognitive organization is relational is unlikely to be rewarded socially with grades regardless of his native ability, the depth of his information, or his background of experience. In fact he will probably be considered deviant and disruptive in the analytically oriented learning environment of the school (p. 830).

Asa Hilliard (1976, p. 41) agrees that the school supports the analytic-cognitive style. Table 3 contrasts schools that would be based upon the analytical and the relational cognitive style.

It is no surprise that Cohen also feels that relational style users are the most creative in the arts. Black children are exposed to a high degree of stimulation from the creative arts. They are surrounded with stimuli from the visual arts, such as posters, paint-

Table 3

The School

As it is in general (Analytical)	As it could be (Relational)
Rules	Freedom
Standardization	Variation
Conformity	Creativity
Memory for specific facts	Memory for essence
Regularity	Novelty
Rigid order	Flexibility
"Normality"	Uniqueness
Differences equal deficits	Sameness equals oppression
Preconceive	Improvise
Precision	Approximate
Logical	Psychological
Atomistic	Global
Egocentric	Sociocentric
Convergent	Divergent
Controlled	Expressive
Meanings are universal	Meanings are contextual
Direct	Indirect
Cognitive	Affective
Linear	Patterned
Mechanical	Humanistic
Unison	Individual in group
Hierarchical	Democratic
Isolation	Integration
Deductive	Inductive
Scheduled	Targets of opportunity
Thing focused	People focused
Constant	Evolving
Sign oriented	Meaning oriented
Duty	Loyalty

(Hilliard 1976, p. 41)

ings, and graffiti; the audio arts, such as phonographs, radios, and tape players; the video arts, such as televisions and films; and the fashion arts, such as creative hairstyles, hats, scarves, and a general orientation toward adornment of the body that grows out of the African heritage.

Another aspect of the creative arts is made up of the performer styles that permeate the Black community. This expressiveness is seen in the behavior of Black preachers, athletes, singers, and dancers and is cultivated in individuals throughout the Black community. The Last Poets, a group of recording artists popular in the early seventies, summed it up by declaring that all Black people "are actors." It is difficult to be Black and boring.

A great deal can be learned about Black culture by analyzing artistic expression.

Black children learn at an early age the significance of perfecting performer roles. Lee Rainwater (1970) discusses Black preschool children's strategies for getting what they want:

> The children learn that they can gain attention by their ability to perform in expressive adult ways, by using the special Black language, by trying seriously to learn the current dances, by imitating hip and cool aspects of adult behavior. Young Black children learn from early childhood the expressive styles of their community (p. 220).

Origins of Cognitive Style

Cohen (1969, p. 831) suggests that children develop their cognitive styles through the socialization they receive in their families and friendship groups. She concludes that children who participate in structured families in "formal" styles of group organization function with analytical cognitive style. Those children who live in more fluid families that she calls "shared-function" primary groups are more likely to utilize relational cognitive styles.

The shared-function group was typical of the low-income community in Pittsburgh that Cohen investigated. She found that the structure and functioning of primary groups in this community were different from typical middle-class groups, and she felt that these differences persisted in spite of ethnic differences among them. She observed that critical functions such as leadership, child care, and the discretionary use of group funds were not assigned to status-roles within the group. Instead, critical functions were periodically performed or shared by all members of the group. This is why they were called "shared-function" primary groups (p. 831).

It appeared that certain kinds of cognitive styles may have developed by day-to-day participation in related kinds of social groups in which the appropriate language structure and methods of thinking about self, things and ideas are necessary components of their related styles of group participation and that these approaches themselves may act to facilitate or impede their "carriers'" ability to become involved in alternate kinds of groups (p. 831).

It is interesting to note that the shared-function primary groups share characteristics of the functioning of Black families (Billingsley 1968, Hill 1972). Black people and lower-income people tend to utilize the relational cognitive style. However, Cohen notes that upper-class people also tend to utilize a predominantly relational style. Although trends have been identified, the use of either style is not confined exclusively to any particular ethnic group or social class. There are different style users in any group. Cohen also discusses the mixtures that occur when a child participates in a family with one mode of functioning and a friendship group with the other pattern.

From this analysis it was possible to isolate four clear response types (p. 834):

1. high-relational pupils who were poor achievers and who had been socialized in, and were at the time of testing, participating in shared-function friendship groups
2. high-analytic pupils who were good achievers and who were socialized in and continued to participate in formally organized primary groups
3. middle-range relational and analytic pupils who were middle-range achievers and who had been socialized in one type of family and were then participating in the other type of friendship group

4. a conflict pattern (high-analytic abstracters but high field dependent) who were middle-range achievers and whose shared-function formal-group style were uniquely mixed

A child's "native ability" does not determine his cognitive style. It shapes the amount of information he knows and his level of abstraction of meaning from an embedding context (for example, reading comprehension or extracting an arithmetic equation from a word problem). Cohen (1969) studied 500 ninth-grade pupils with an intelligence range from "barely educable" to "gifted" and found sharp differences between the barely educable and the gifted in the numbers of the information components of their test scores. Similar large differences were found in the levels of abstraction they used. Cohen found that "both types of differences appeared on all measures of ability and performance regardless of which conceptual style the pupils used. Native ability, then, may be better defined as the differential ability of individuals to absorb large bodies of information and to reach high levels of abstraction using *either* mode of conceptual organization" (p. 838).

Nonverbal Tests of Intelligence

In an attempt to be culturally fair in assessing intelligence, some psychologists have devised tests they call "culture free." They have eliminated components that measure "information growth." It is felt that assessing the depth of information of a child is really measuring the extent to which he has been exposed to the culture rather than his intellectual ability. The "culture free" tests are nonverbal and supposedly measure the ability to reason "logically." However, Cohen (1969, p. 840) argues that these tests composed of logical sequences are more culture-bound than the information tests and favor the child with an analytical cognitive style that is typically found among Anglo-American middle-class children. The ability to solve the sequences presented requires that the child utilize a parts-specific, stimulus-centered, analytic mode of abstraction. A relational pupil who is well informed and widely experienced and who doesn't utilize the analytic style would score poorly on the test. At least with tests that measure information growth or depth of exposure to the culture, one would find some relational children who would score well. As a matter of fact, Cohen argues,

The most intelligent relational pupils score the worst of all. Their ability to reach higher levels of abstraction through relational pathways takes them farther away from the higher levels of abstraction reached through analytic pathways. . . . Highly intelligent high-relational pupils were found, in fact, to communicate best with the demands of the school on the concrete level. . . . It appears, therefore, that given concrete settings with intelligence held constant, high-relational pupils can compete with analytic ones. It is only when high levels of analytic abstraction are required that their ability to compete is inhibited (pp. 840–41).

Cohen also found that relational and analytic students communicate best with each other on the concrete level. The greatest gaps in communication occur between the most intelligent members of the two categories (p. 841).

Her findings, in summary, are these: "Nonverbal tests of intelligence have not freed themselves from their culture-bound characteristics. Instead, they have focused on one critical aspect of culture—its method of selecting and organizing relevant sense data" (p. 841). These nonverbal tests of intelligence are much more discriminatory against relational pupils than the instruments they were designed to replace.

Cohen also clarifies the terminology that has been used to describe the difficulties of low-income children with tests and performance on analytic tasks (p. 838). "Culture difference" occurs when children have not had experiences that provide them with the kind of information that is usable in school. A child might have a storehouse of information, but it is not the background that is required for the school curriculum. "Culture conflict" occurs when the child is using a learning style that differs from the analytic learning and behavioral style reinforced in the school.

Certain features of the relational and analytic modes make it difficult for a child to develop characteristics that are present in the other mode. Learned behavior, language, interpersonal patterns, values, beliefs and general cultural context of a person determine his cognitive style. This comprehensive context from which the child operates promotes one style of learning and suppresses the other (p. 839).

In their study of what they call the "hard-core" poor, Cohen, Fraenkel and Brewer (1968) found incompatibility with analytic abstraction in three categories of thought:

1. *perceptions of time* (These children perceived of time as a series of discrete moments rather than as a continuum.)
2. *perception of self* in social space (They considered themselves to be in the center of space rather than in a position relative to others who are passing together at different rates of speed through social space.)
3. *causality* (They perceived specific causality of events rather than multiple causality.)

They state further that the analytic mode of abstraction presumes the universe to be organized in a linear fashion: time is a continuum; social space is a linear hierarchy; and events result from multiple causality. This assumption of linearity is not found among relational children on tests of cognitive style. It is neither present in their language style nor in patterns of ordering authority or responsibility in their shared-function social groups.

These researchers suggest that the analytic conception of linearity gives rise to values and beliefs that create culture conflict for relational children.

For instance, without the assumption of linearity such notions as social mobility, the value of money, improving one's performance, getting ahead, infinity, or hierarchies of any type, all of which presume the linear extension of critical elements, do not have meaning for the relational child. In essence, the requirements for formal abstraction and extension of critical elements do not have meaning for the relational child. In essence, the requirements for formal abstraction and extraction of components to produce linear continua are not logically possible within the relational rule-set (p. 839).

I am not convinced by the foregoing examples, particularly that relational children don't value money, improving one's performance, and getting ahead. However, the analysis that relational children do not conceive of the world as organized in a linear fashion may have validity.

Afro-American Cultural Style

It is interesting to note that aspects of African and Afro-American culture have been described as organized in a circular fashion in contrast to the linear organization of Western culture (Borneman 1959, Abrahams 1970).

Borneman suggests that a circular approach to music and language is a dominant feature of Afro-American culture:

While the whole European tradition strives for regularity of pitch, of time, of timbre and of vibrato—the African tradition strives precisely for the negation of these elements. In language, the African tradition aims at circumlocution rather than at exact definition. The direct statement is considered crude and unimaginative; the veiling of all contents in ever-changing paraphrases is considered the criterion of intelligence and personality. In music, the same tendency towards obliquity and ellipsis is noticeable: no note is attacked straight; the voice or instrument always approaches it from above or below, plays around the implied pitch without ever remaining on it for any length of time, and departs from it without ever having committed itself to a single meaning (p. 17).

Roger Abrahams (p. 8) also identifies the African and Afro-American musical style as circular as compared with the linear western style. The following is an excerpt from a chart that illustrates his analysis:

African and Afro-American	Western
Circular, vertiginal organization of performing group; heavy emphasis on involvement through repetition of sound and movement; episodic arrangement calling for small, short units leading to a succession of mini-climaxes; retreat from closure in favor of the on-going and open-ended (*running the changes*).	Linear, progressive organization, driving toward climax and catharsis (insight and relief of tension); repetition not valued; when it occurs employed for intensifying tension. Very strong demand for closure.

It is appropriate that we consider circularity (relational) and linearity (analytic) as they are expressed in the arts because artistic expression is inextricably bound to the way one conceptualizes the universe. This is particularly true of African culture. Bohannon (1964) states that "art permeates African culture, which in turn permeates African art. Art is not set aside from 'real life'—it cannot be among a people who do not make such distinctions" (p. 150).

The place of the arts in African culture from which Afro-Americans came is different from the definition of the arts in Euro-American culture, as Alan Merriam (1958) describes:

The stress placed upon musical activity as an integral and functioning part of the society is a feature that music shares with other aesthetic aspects of culture in Africa and one which is emphasized in almost all non-literate societies. In Euro-American society, in contrast, there is a tendency to compartmentalize the arts and divorce them from aspects of everyday life; thus we have 'pure' art as opposed to 'applied' art, as well as the 'artist' and 'commercial artist' or 'craftsman,' who are also differentiated both in role and in function. A further distinction is made in Western society in terms of 'artist' and 'audience,' with the first group tending to be limited in number. . . . Relatively large numbers of people within [African] society are competent in the arts, and aesthetic activities are closely related to the whole functioning culture (pp. 49–50).

Roger Abrahams (1970, p. 8) describes differences in Afro-American and Euro-American performer/audience styles that illustrate the pervasiveness of artistic expression in the Black community. He says that creative vitality comes from a source outside the individual. This energy is called into play by the performer and his performance. The individual performer is regarded as the instigator of action only. He is not appreciated necessarily because he is so much more talented than the group. He is appreciated for his ability to bring the group into the performance, thus sharing the energy source.

In contrast, in Euro-American culture creative vitality comes from within the performer. His energies and abilities are drawn out and focused upon by the audience. He is appreciated for his virtuosity. He leads them by the hand.

It is not surprising that Singleton (1969) says the relational conceptual style has given rise to people who are more creative and expressive in the arts than those who use the analytic style.

Asa Hilliard (1976, pp. 38–39) has described the core of Afro-American cultural style:

1. Afro-American people tend to respond to things in terms of the whole picture instead of its parts. The Euro-American tends to believe that anything can be divided and subdivided into pieces and that these pieces add up to a whole. Therefore, art is sometimes taught by numbers, as are dancing and music. That is why some people never learn to dance. They are too busy counting and analyzing.
2. Afro-American people tend to prefer inferential reasoning to deductive or inductive reasoning.
3. Afro-American people tend to approximate space, numbers, and time rather than stick to accuracy.
4. Afro-American people tend to prefer to focus on people and their activities rather than on things. This tendency is shown by the fact that so many Black students choose careers in the helping professions, such as teaching, psychology, social work, and so forth, even though a scarcity of jobs exist in those areas and the curriculum is not particularly easy.
5. Afro-American people have a keen sense of justice and are quick to analyze and perceive injustice.
6. Afro-American people tend to lean toward altruism, a concern for one's fellow man.
7. Afro-American people tend to prefer novelty, freedom, and personal distinctiveness. This is shown in the development of improvisations in music and styles of clothing.
8. Afro-American people in general tend not to be "word" dependent. They tend to be very proficient in nonverbal communications.

A strong relationship exists between Afro-American cultural styles and Cohen's relational style.

Dr. Na'im Akbar* has also proposed a description of the Afro-American child. (See Table 4.) Note the similarities in his description to the foregoing analysis.

Table 4

The Afro-American Child

Is highly affective.
Uses language requiring a wide use of many coined interjections (sometimes profanity).
Expresses herself or himself through considerable body language.
Relies on words that depend upon context for meaning and that have little meaning in themselves.
Prefers using expressions that have meaning connotations.
Adopts a systematic use of nuances of intonation and body language, such as eye movement and positioning.
Prefers oral-aural modalities for learning communication.
Is highly sensitive to others' nonverbal cues.
Seeks to be people oriented.
Is sociocentric.
Uses internal cues for problem solving.
Feels highly empathetic.
Likes spontaneity.
Adapts rapidly to novel stimuli.

(Akbar 1975)

Asa Hilliard (1976) relates an example of how an analytical person would function on a relational task:

If this person were asked to learn an Afro-American dance, the analytical is "very likely to draw feet on the floor and to break the dance down into steps and to try to learn the dance 'piecemeal.' It is also likely that the analytical will establish a 'standard' of performance which becomes 'right' or 'not right.' On the other hand, if a relational is given an analytical task, a comparable translation will take place. Details are likely to be blurred, standards faintly adhered to or the dance itself may be modified with no real concern for right or wrong so much as 'fit' or 'harmony' " (p. 42).

If it is a square dance, that dance, according to Hilliard, is likely to be given rhythm or some other expression of individual creativity. An example is The Wiz, a Broadway show that is a Black version of the Anglo-American story The Wonderful Wizard of Oz. Another example is the change that was made by Africans in the square dance popular in the southern United States when it was carried back to

*Quoted by Hilliard (1976, p. 39).

Liberia by Afro-Americans. It has rhythm, freedom, improvisation, and expression. These types of transformations are usually made with any cultural form interacted with: language, religion, music, humor, art, and so forth.

In summary, here are some basic assumptions that Hilliard has suggested about human behavioral styles:

1. A behavioral style is a framework from which a person views the world.
2. Several styles can be described. At one extreme is the analytic and at the other extreme is the relational, with other possible styles on a continuum between.
3. A person may change his or her basic style by learning aspects of other styles.
4. Since styles are the framework from which one views the world, the style can be observed in all areas of his expression, such as through his world view, language, music, religion, art, work, dance, problem solving, sports, writing, or any other area of human expression.
5. Some relationship exists between style and socioeconomic level.
6. A strong relationship exists between style and cultural or ethnic group membership, especially where a given ethnic group is located at a traditional point on the socioeconomic scale.
7. No evidence exists of a relationship between basic intelligence and style. Able people are found to the same degree among all style users.
8. Every style is necessary, valuable, and useful in human experience if society is to function fully.
9. A "gifted" person is one who has integrated and harmonized the different styles within himself or herself to focus one harmonized style.

Three

Culture and Child-Rearing

Now there rose up a king over Egypt which knew not Joseph.

—Exodus 1:8

Pharaoh became alarmed at the rapid increases in the numbers of Hebrew slaves. He issued a decree that all male Hebrew babies were to be cast into the water at birth. A man in the tribe of Levi took a wife who bore a child during this time. She hid the child for three months; then, unable to conceal him any longer, she made a basket and let him float near the bank of the river. His sister Miriam watched the child and ensured his safety.

Each day the daughter of Pharaoh came down to wash herself at this river. She saw the basket and asked her maidens to fetch it. When she opened it, the baby wept. She said with compassion, "This is one of the Hebrews' children." At that moment, Miriam, the baby's sister, emerged from the bulrushes and said, "Shall I go and call a nurse of the Hebrew women so that she may nurse the child for you?" And Pharaoh's daughter said to her, "Go." Miriam went and called the child's mother, Hannah, and Pharaoh's daughter said to her, "Take this child away and nurse it for me, and I will give you wages." And the woman took the child and nursed it.

And the child grew, and the woman brought him unto Pharaoh's daughter. He became her son, and she called him Moses.

But even though Moses grew up in the house of Pharaoh and became his son, there was a difference between Moses and the other sons of Pharaoh. Pharaoh's sons grew up to become oppressors, but Moses grew up to become a liberator. The difference between Moses and Pharaoh's sons was the difference made by Moses' nurse, who was his mother. Moses' mother not only nursed him with the milk of her breast, but she also imbued her child with a clear understanding of who he was, who the enemy was, and what he must do. She provided Moses with an identity, a god, and a heritage so that when his moment in history arrived and he saw an

The task of the Black family has been to prepare its children to live and be among white people without becoming *white people.*

Egyptian overseer striking a Hebrew slave, he did not experience an identity crisis. He immediately knew whose side he was on and what had to be done. Without Hannah, there would have been no Moses.

Wade Nobles (1975) has pointed out that the task of the Black family has been to prepare its children to live and be among white people without *becoming* white people. No formal "Black studies" program has existed in this country to tell Black people who they are. But just as Moses' mother, Hannah, taught him who Joseph was as well as who Abraham, Isaac and Jacob were, Black mothers taught their children who Booker T. Washington was and who Phyllis Wheatley, Harriet Tubman, W. E. B. DuBois, and Marian Anderson were. When the news media projected Martin Luther King in a dubious light during the early civil rights movement and questioned his tactics and leadership, it was Black mothers who turned off the television sets and interpreted the meaning of Martin Luther King and the struggle for Black children.

It is appropriate that we devote special attention to the relationship between the Black woman and her child because of the strong bond that exists between them. As Nobles (1974b, p. 15) has pointed out, the special bond cannot be attributed merely to the fact that slavery legally defined the family as mother and child, but it is "deeply rooted in our African heritage and philosophical orientation which ... places a special value on children because they represent the continuity of life." Robert Bell has suggested that motherhood has been historically an important role for Black women, possibly even more important than the role of wife. Also imperative is that our consideration of the Black woman and child-rearing proceed within the context of our Africanity and from the perspective of our African heritage.

Historically, research on the Black woman has paralleled or has been a part of research on the Black family that has defined her as domineering, pathological, and matriarchal. We must join the scholars who interpret the Black woman in terms of Black (African) social reality. Joyce Ladner (1971), for example, has pointed out that it is more appropriate to describe the Black woman as *strong* than to describe her as domineering. This strength has contributed immeasurably to our survival, for she has had to maintain the dual role of working for wages and shouldering the primary responsibility for the household.

During slavery, women were often forced to work as hard as men, even during pregnancy. After childbirth, when they suffered from full breasts because the infant could not join them in the fields to nurse, many of them were beaten raw by the overseer when they did not keep up with the men (Davis, 1971). But even though childbirth has imposed varying degrees of hardship on them, women have struggled through infant mortality, forced abortions, forced sterilizations, informal adoptions, and planned parenthood propaganda to produce children for the survival of the Black race.

Robert B. Hill (1972) suggests that "the preoccupation with pathology in most research on Black families has obscured some fruitful avenues of investigation." He contends that examining the strengths of Black families can contribute as much toward understanding and ameliorating social problems as examining their weaknesses. He suggests further that "if, as most scholars agree, there is a need to strengthen Black families, then a first-order priority should be the identification of presently existing strengths and resources." Dr. Hill identifies and analyzes five such strengths: strong kinship bonds, strong achievement orientation, adaptability of family roles, strong religious orientation, and strong work orientation. He maintains that these five characteristics have been functional for the survival, advancement, and stability of Black families.

In his pioneering work on African continuities in the Black family, Wade Nobles (1974b) has presented evidence that suggests the African-American family's "definition, character, form, and function did not begin with the American experience of slavery, and as a system it has an historical continuation extending back in history to traditional Africa and its culture" (pp. 3, 4).

Strong Kinship Bonds

In considering the strong kinship bonds of Black families identified by Hill, Nobles (1974b, p. 12) has pointed out its African context. Two guiding principles characterize the African ethos: survival of the tribe and the oneness of being. A deep sense of family or kinship characterizes African social reality. This family system is described by Mbiti (1970) as vertical in that it includes the living and the dead and those unborn, and horizontal in that it includes all living persons in the tribe even though they are in different family units.

Nobles argues that the strong mutual-aid orientation and kinship bonds found in Black families are derived from the African heritage.

Robert Staples (1974) writes about the parakinship ties in the Black community wherein Blacks refer to each other as "sister," "brother," "cousin," "blood brother," or "homeboy" to imply a family closeness when no real kinship exists. A strong desire exists among Black people to be related to each other.

Hill (1972, pp. 6–7) points out that while few Blacks utilize formal adoption mechanisms, an informal system of adoption operates in the Black community. Many Blacks were raised completely or for periods of time by an aunt or a grandmother or a next-door neighbor. Black women tend not to surrender their children for adoption to agencies as readily as white women, and when it is necessary, they more frequently tend to adopt each other's children.

Dr. Nobles (1974b, pp. 13–14) suggests that the African ethos (survival of the tribe and oneness of being) and the African philosophical principles (collective responsibility and cooperative work) are related to this sense of kinship: "Is not the practice of 'ain't none of my children no better than the others' an expression of the 'oneness of being,' and is not the practice of informal adoption, 'one more child ain't gonna make no difference' a (n) . . . expression of survival of the tribe and collective responsibility?" (p. 10.)

Achievement Orientation

Black parents have always stressed to their children the importance of their exceeding white children's behavior and performance because falling short would reflect unfavorably upon the group. Black children usually are given very strict guidelines for behavior on the bus or in public because loudness and boisterousness could make white people feel that all Blacks are that way.

Robert Hill has identified a strong achievement orientation as a strength of Black families. He cites as evidence that most of the Black youths in college come from families who were not college educated. This suggests that many Black parents are sacrificing to provide for their children a college education they never had.

A study (Polling the Children, *Time* 1977) by Temple University investigated what life looks like for an elementary school child. An interesting finding was that more than 75 percent of the Black children and 66 percent of the whites said that their mother wanted them to be "one of the best students in the class."

Several researchers (Radin 1970, Sandis 1970, Bell 1965) have investigated the relationship between the aspirations of Black mothers and the achievement of Black children.

Norma Radin (1970, pp. 1–11) investigated the relationship between maternal practices as observed in the home and the cognitive development of young children from low-income families. The purpose of the study was to determine whether lower-income maternal warmth was associated with the intellectual growth of the child. The findings revealed that in lower-class families maternal use of reinforcement, consultation with the child, and sensitivity to his feelings appear to be conducive to the intellectual growth of the preschool child. One major intervening variable she found was the arousal of the child's motivation to achieve, possibly by affecting his desire to please adults, his desire to explore his environment, or both. Radin recommends further research in this area because the results of this study indicate that maternal child-rearing practices significantly affect a child's response to an educational program. Most educational reform focuses upon curriculum modification or restructuring the public school system. She maintains that maternal child-rearing practices should not be overlooked in considering educational reform (p. 11).

Eva Sandis (1970, pp. 204–11) examined the extent to which specific socialization techniques are associated with the transmission of mother's educational ambitions for their children and the children's own educational plans. This relationship was present regardless of the extent to which they provided the students with culturally enriching activities, pressured them to do well in school, or kept in touch with the schools. Sandis interprets the findings as indicating that parental values are transmitted in many ways other than by specific behaviors. What the mother desires for her children is more critical than what she does. This may add credence to the adage: "More is caught than taught!"

R. R. Bell (1965) suggests a range of beliefs and values among Black lower-class mothers. He also has found some deviation between the stated aspirations of the mother and specific values that would be thought to lead toward the realization of those aspirations. This deviation is particularly present among mothers of the lowest income levels. For example, a mother might aspire for her children to achieve high educational and occupational goals but at the same time express the thought that they should marry young and have a large family. An implicit contradiction exists because one would expect that those mothers who have high educational and occupational aspirations for their children would also expect them to marry at an older age and to have fewer children. An implication of this study might be that lower-income mothers have high aspirations for their children but little understanding of the steps necessary for attaining the goals.

Interesting to investigate is the reason for so many lower-income Black children's achievements that surpass those of their parents even though they apparently had meager support and resources. In contrast, many middle-class children who apparently had substantial support from their parents fell below the accomplishments of their parents in their own adult achievement status.

Howard Thurman,* a noted Black philosopher and theologian, has postulated the construct of the "humbling negative" in his book *The Centering Moment.* He suggests that one draws strength through struggle. Drawing upon this construct, we might analyze that the unsatisfied desires of lower-income children might result in greater motivation to achieve than is present in some middle-class children who take for granted the life-style they enjoy.

Harriette McAdoo (1979) has identified an upward mobility pattern in Black families. She calls a couple first generation if they have significant occupational or educational upward mobility in comparison with their parents. Even though she does not account for the factors that precipitate this achievement, she says they are able to transmit to their children a strong motivation to achieve; therefore, the second generation maintains a comparable level of achievement. Middle-class status is so tenuous in the Black community that parents are not able to accumulate inheritances to pass

---

*Quoted in a sermon by Dr. Joseph Roberts at Ebenezeer Baptist Church, Atlanta, Georgia, 1977.

on to their children; so they invest in education and spur their children on to achievement and ultimate independence. However, apparently the third-generation children cannot remember the "plantation," and a decline occurs in their achievement below the level of the first and second generations.

M. L. Maehr (1974) suggests that the motivation to achieve is present among children of all cultures, no matter the way in which it is directed. He suggests that study should be done of the circumstances under which children "turn on" to the school curriculum and then integrate aspects of those situations into other areas of the curriculum or program. He feels that it may be more fruitful for intervention strategies to focus upon changing the situation rather than the child.

We must learn to identify the ends to which different cultures motivate children to achieve. A child might be highly motivated to achieve in athletics, for example, but not as motivated to achieve in other areas valued by the culture. Maehr claims that "current assessment procedures are so culturally bound that they only sample instances of achievement motivation associated with a given culture" (p. 894).

A casual observation of a few Black athletes reveals that older brothers provided the models for some outstanding athletes. Often the elder brothers did not achieve fame, but the younger brothers benefited from the experience and motivation the elder brothers were able to transmit. In a television interview Floyd Patterson admitted that although his two older brothers were boxers, he was the first to "make it big." Archie Griffin, a two-time Heisman trophy winner, comes from a large family of males. Even though his older brothers were good football players, there was a marked improvement in his skills as well as those of his younger brothers. This analysis may also hold for those athletes who do not have older brothers; older boys in their communities might serve the aforementioned modeling function.

Manuel Ramirez and Douglas Price-Williams (1976, pp. 49–60) conducted a study of achievement motivation in children of three ethnic groups in the United States—Anglos, Blacks, and Mexican-Americans. They sought to determine whether motivation to achieve was related to a need the child felt within himself or whether it stemmed from a motivation to please his family. The results showed that the Mexican-American and Black children scored higher on family achievement than did the Anglo children. The Anglo children scored higher on achievement related to their self needs. The females in all three ethnic groups scored lower on self-need achievement but higher on family achievement than the males. The study concluded that "contextual conditions are most important in expression of achievement motivation and that the particular form in which achievement is expressed is determined by the definition that culture gives to it" (p. 49).

Adaptability of Family Roles

Hill (1972) has identified adaptability of family roles as a strength of Black families. Nobles (1974a and b) relates this also to the African principles of cooperative work and collective responsibility. According to their analysis, in Black families relations are egalitarian. Women are often employed, and men share the responsibility for child care. Older children also participate in many instances by sharing in care of young siblings and working jobs outside the home to contribute to the support of the family.

Strong Religious Orientation

Black child-rearing has a strong religious orientation. Na'im Akbar (1975) observed in a speech that Black women "didn't know nothin' 'bout Dr. Spock, but they did know the Bible—'raise up a child in the way he should go and when he is old he will not depart from it."

As Robert Hill points out, even though the strong religious orientation of Black families is widely discussed, it has almost never been documented empirically. Furthermore, Hill's and other discussions of the Black church focus primarily upon the political role of the church during slavery and the civil rights movement.

The church's economic leadership is demonstrated by the leadership of Rev. Leon Sullivan, the founder of the Opportunities Industrialization Center (OIC), one of the first community-sponsored job training programs, which began with the contributions of Sullivan's parishioners. Another example of economic leadership is that of Rev. Jesse Jackson, the president of People United to Save Humanity (PUSH).

Other studies of the Black church focus on the emotional quality of the services and the spiritual release the parishioners receive as they dream of "pie in the sky by and by."

However, very little attention has been given to the role of the Black church as a socializing institution. W. E. B. DuBois (1899) has produced one of the most significant works that examines that role of the Black church.

DuBois claims that the Black church is the center of social intercourse to a degree unknown in white churches. He describes the life of an individual or family that is closely involved in the church as somehow different from those who do not have that involvement. Church membership is not limited to Sunday morning contact at worship services. It provides children and adults with a peer group. The organizations and activities of the church give Black people an opportunity to provide leadership and to exhibit and develop competencies that are not available in the broader society. Thus, we have a woman who is a domestic worker all week, who at church is the president of the missionary society. Or we have a man who is a janitor all week but at church is a member of the Trustee Board and obtains expertise in financial matters.

Comparable experiences are provided for children growing up in the church. Entertainment and athletics are two of the means by which Black youths have been able to achieve wealth and enhanced status. However, little recognition is given to the fact that the church is the training ground for Black musicians. Children gain experience and training through singing in the church choirs. Some move into semisecular groups, such as gospel groups, and others move directly into rhythm and blues. An example is Aretha Franklin, who is a preacher's daughter; Isaac Hayes; The Staples Singers; and countless others.

So the church is the hub of social life for those involved. Black women participate in the largest numbers in church worship and activities. Often the question is raised of how Black women who are single can manage so well in raising their children alone. The answer is they are not alone. The church provides a kind of extended family fellowship that provides other significant adults to relate to the children, and it also provides material and human resources to the family.

Jeanne Giovanni and Andrew Billingsley (1970) conducted a study to identify factors that might differentiate between lower-income mothers who were neglectful of their children and more adequate mothers. They asked questions of the mothers of three ethnic groups (Black, Caucasian, and Spanish-speaking) to determine their levels of information about and participation in various community structures: church; political systems; and various social systems, including public utilities, recreational facilities, medical care, housing, education, and welfare.

The only area they found to be significantly related to the mother's functioning was in church attendance.

Although the church is a formal community structure, church activities often bring members into closer informal contacts. This was so of many of the women, particularly the black mothers who reported attending church functions other than worship service. In general, the adequate mothers were much more engaged with the church than were the less adequate. The church was prob-

ably a source of support to these women, and possibly an untapped resource of assistance for neglectful parents (p. 201).

Giovanni and Billingsley note that it is important to evaluate families within the context of their ethnic groups. They found clear ethnic variations in the area of kinship relations, functioning in formal social systems, and in child-rearing practices (p. 202).

Strong Work Orientation

Robert Hill (1972) has documented the fact that Black families place a strong emphasis on work and ambition. He suggests that most Black families have double earners (wife and husband providing income). Also, the Black poor are more likely to work than the white poor. We will explore the strong work orientation of Black families in the section on the socialization of male and female children in Afro-American culture.

African Child-Rearing

A limited number of studies have been conducted that examine characteristics of African society and values transmitted through socialization. Most of the available research is deficit-oriented and is written from the colonizer's perspective. Five studies are presented here as examples of research from which positive information can be obtained as well as suggestions for areas of future study. This is not intended to be an exhaustive treatment of African child-rearing but rather a sampling of efforts in a positive direction that may have implications for Afro-American child-rearing.

The first study, by Helen Green (1971), shows similarities between the values of West African and Caribbean women, adding credence to the argument that continuities exist among people of African heritage even though they are dispersed throughout the world. The second study, by Robert and Ruth Munroe (1977), describes the manner in which Kenyan culture (in East Africa) develops cooperation in children and contrasts that with the way the culture of the United States cultivates competition in Anglo children. The third study by Robert and Ruth Munroe and Robert Daniels (1976) examines the type of economy found in Kenya and analyzes the relationships among the economy, the resultant socialization practices, and the functioning of children on a cognitive task. The fourth and fifth studies by Akpan Ebsen (1973) and Austin Shelton (1968) describe child-rearing in Nigeria.

Helen Green (1971) studied three groups of lower-income expectant women—West African, Caribbean, and East Indian—to determine their preferences of behavior by their children. The West-

African sample was drawn from Gambia (between Senegal and Guinea); the Caribbean women were Negroes in Trinidad; and the East Indians were living in Trinidad.

The responses were organized into three categories that reflect values in the socialization of children:

1. *Social Breadth* is defined as a value indicated by preference for behavior that shows concern for and interaction with many people rather than only a few persons. The following kinds of responses reflect this value:
   a. priority given by mother to other members of the family or to friends at the time when a child wants attention
   b. trust for child care placed by mother in nonrelatives
   c. willingness by the mother for or benefit considered to derive from interaction of the child with nonrelatives
2. *Autonomy* is defined as a value that prefers behavior showing individual action divorced from others. The following kinds of responses reflect this value:
   a. mother's encouragement of early self-care on the part of the child
   b. mother's emphasis on early self-reliance by the child
   c. mother's use of concrete rewards and punishments for reinforcement, that is, offering or restricting objects and activities, as contrasted with mother's behavior suggesting conditional love or love withdrawal as a means of control
3. *Expressionism* is defined as a value that prefers spontaneous behavior. It indicates an avoidance of postponement or repression. While expressionism may secondarily involve a lack of willful control, it is primarily determined by a positive preference for clear, unreserved, and uncomplicated behavior. The following kinds of responses are considered to reflect this value:
   a. less emphasis by mothers on delay of gratification
   b. less emphasis by mothers on denial of impulse
   c. less emphasis by mothers on "good character" and rectitude (pp. 310–11).

The findings of the study revealed that the three groups of mothers differed significantly from each other on *social breadth*. The Trinidadian mothers ranked first, the West African mothers ranked second, and the East Indian mothers were distinctly lower than the other two groups in their support of this value.

The West African and Trinidadian mothers did not differ significantly from each other on *autonomy*, but each differed from the East Indian sample. The West African mothers ranked highest, the Trinidadian mothers were a close second, and the East Indian mothers were distinctly lower in support of this value.

The three groups of mothers differed significantly from each other on *expressionism*. The West African mothers ranked highest, the Trinidadian mothers were a close second, and the East Indian mothers were distinctly lower in their support of this value (pp. 311–12).

The observers were impressed by the similarity in behavior among the West Africans and Trinidadians, who originally shared the same culture. The differences between those two groups and the East Indians were striking. The East Indians seem to have totally different behavior patterns even though they have lived for a century and a half as an equally large subculture with the Blacks in Trinidad, a Caribbean island colonized by the British. This study clearly indicates the persistence of cultural patterns in the African diaspora (p. 310).

Helen Green also interpreted the findings of this study in relationship to the cultural expectations for the behavior of women in these three cultures:

The results are congruent with what each culture expects of women or permits them in contacts outside the home, self-directed activities, and psychological equality with men. In contrast to East Indian women, the West African and Trinidadian women develop flexibility through early responsibilities, trading experience, and decision-making in their homes (p. 300).

Robert Munroe and Ruth Munroe (1977, pp. 145–46) examined cooperation versus competition among rural/traditional children and among urban/industrial children. They compared Kikuyu children from a peri-urban, semitraditional community in Kenya with suburban United States children.

A comparison was made of the performance of the children on a board game. The goal of the game could be reached more effectively through subtle cooperation than through competition.

They concluded that the African children were more cooperative than the American children because of the socialization they receive. Socialization in sub-Saharan Africa universally emphasizes strong pressures toward compliance. This compliance training has been found to affect both conformity and obedience. The findings of this study indicate that cooperative behavior may also be affected by compliance training.

The Kikuyu children are involved in daily work activities in which they are requested by their parents to cooperate with others and comply with requests that offer no immediate tangible rewards (such as helping to carry firewood) or that provide rewards but are shared (such as assisting with food preparation). The investigators suggest that this type of chore-performance produced by demanding compliance from a child may also teach the cooperative or turn-taking behavior that is shown in the board-game task of this study.

In comparison Munroe and Munroe found that the American children received a socialization that provided work experiences of a less cooperative nature. Their socialization emphasized individual rewards. Therefore, in the board-game task of the study they were less successful in reaching the goal because of the subtle cooperation required.

Robert Munroe, Ruth Munroe and Robert Daniels (1976, pp. 133–34) explained the relationship between the type of economy an East African society engaged in, the resultant socialization practices, and the functioning of the children on a cognitive task. They contrasted societies that engaged in three types of economic activities: agricultural, hunting-gathering, and herding. They found that societies engaged in herding emphasized compliance in children (as compared to assertion) because the food supply had to be tended carefully during the year. Societies that were agriculturally based emphasized compliance to a lesser extent, and those who were hunters were much less likely to do so.

Kenyan cultures were examined. They were defined as herding on the basis of the number of cattle in the communities from which the children were drawn. The children were then given a cognitive test that was a standard Piagetian assessment of acquiring the conservation of mass. These investigators found that the herding society that emphasized severe compliance training produced children who performed less effectively on the cognitive task. The subjects from the agriculturally based society were significantly better on the conservation task.

Akpan Ebsen (1973) analyzes the child-rearing practices found in Nigeria to point out global differences in the culture between the United States and Africa. He maintains there are differences in the attitudes and modes of interaction in interpersonal relationships in these two cultures. He refers to the clusters of African attitudes and modes of response as the *Care Syndrome.*

Ebsen describes the Africans as his brother's keeper. He grows up in a small rural community for the most part and is imbued from early childhood with an empathetic concern for his fellows. In contrast, people who grow up in Western societies often do not know their neighbors and have detached urban attitudes. They do not know what it means to care about the people in their communities or to offer help to those even in desperate need of help (pp. 205–6).

Ebsen suggests that the African modes of child-rearing give rise to the development of humane attitudes and the care syndrome. Unlike western child-rearing, African socialization emphasizes the closeness of man to man. Physical and psychological closeness is reinforced by encouragement of body contact between people (p. 207).

The African child receives more body contact than his Western counterpart. Most children are breast-fed and for longer periods of time than in other societies. Before and after a child learns to walk, he spends a great deal of time being held by his mother on her lap or being carried on her back or the back of an older sibling. Usually the child sleeps with his mother during infancy until a new baby arrives. The African child learns early in his childhood to embrace relatives and friends in greeting them or thanking them for a special favor. Thus, the child grows up in a social network characterized by physical closeness, acceptance, and care. He expects to receive affection and comfort and learns to give it when it is needed by others.

By the time an African child is six years old, he begins to take responsibility for providing care for a younger sibling. He carries the child on his back, cradles the child on his lap, and learns to respond with body contact and carrying behavior to fit the various needs of the child (p. 207).

Ebsen concludes that in Western society objects come between the child and his mother. The babies are more prone to be bottle-fed, carried around in baby carriages, placed in playpens to play alone, and placed in a separate bed for sleeping. These gadgets come physically between the baby and his mother's body and interfere with the physical and psychological body warmth provided in Africa (p. 208).

From the African viewpoint, the Western child is socialized into a life of detachment and impersonality. These early attitudes are reinforced by the urban environment. People are seen as things in the distance or numbers in the computer. A basic aloofness is developed toward people that begins with the distance from the mother created by the bottle and the baby carriage (p. 208).

Ebsen suggests that the *care syndrome* is reflected in the use of language among African people. One key indicator he describes is the method of greeting and other polite exchanges. Africans have elaborate greetings for nearly every kind of situation. Foreigners are often astounded by the elaborateness and emotionalism of African greetings. The greeting always includes inquiries about people who are important to the person being greeted.

Western greetings are less effusive; the greeter usually discusses the weather and rarely inquires about human life and conditions. "The closest they ever seem to come to some concern for the individual is 'How are you?' And even that in American usage has become impersonalized into a mere 'Hi' " (p. 208).

Among African people, when a gift is acknowledged, the recipient offers thanks as well as a kind wish to the giver. (An example cited by Ebsen is *Sosongo*, meaning *May you grow stronger* in the Efik language, spoken in southeastern Nigeria.) In the English language often one merely offers thanks to the giver in what sometimes becomes an impersonal business transaction.

Ebsen states further that African children grow up speaking a language that expresses caring and feeling to a greater extent than Western children; therefore, they are prone to develop the attitude of caring since their lifestyle encourages those feelings (p. 209).

The extended family system supports the care syndrome. A little girl, for example, comes to see parents, grandparents, uncles, aunts, and cousins as a part of her everyday life. Every older person participates in caring for her and all have claims on her concern and care. The survival of the family depends upon how the members care about and provide for each other.

This situation usually does not exist in Western culture. The nuclear family structure of father-mother-child does not encourage this extended caring network. Usually parents are eager for their teenage children to live on their own and solve their own problems. The children in turn are eager to live on their own as soon as possible. Grandparents usually must fend for themselves during their last helpless years or be sent to old people's homes surrounded by strange people and impersonal relationships. Thus, children are deprived of the nurture they could have received from grandparents (p. 209).

The extended family system also provides the child with a number of male models found in fathers, uncles, grown-up brothers, and cousins. Thus, if their father is absent they have other men in the household to relate to and identify with (p. 209).

The analysis of Austin Shelton (1968) regarding Igbo child-rearing in eastern Nigeria supports the observations of Ebsen. He describes dependence as a virtue. Each age-group is interdependent to the extent that a network is created among children, parents, grandparents, and ancestors on a vertical plane and extended family relatives and members of other families on a horizontal plane.

Ruth and Robert Munroe (1975) found that among the Logoli, the infants in large-membership households were held more and were responded to more than were infants in households with fewer members.

Africans in the Caribbean

Otterbein (1973, p. 1670) investigated the effect of supernatural beliefs of Black people in the Bahama islands on child-rearing practices. The hypothesis was that caretakers who fear the supernatural will inflict more pain on children in their charge than those caretakers who do not fear the supernatural. This hypothesis is drawn from a larger body of theory that states that child training practices influence adult personality, including beliefs in the supernatural. Those beliefs influence the training of children.

The investigator identified three realms of the supernatural belief system: 1) All believe in the Christian deity. They believe that God helps people; a few believe that God hurts or punishes as much as he helps. All mothers or grandmothers tell their charges that if they are bad, God will punish them. 2) The second realm is that of spirits of the dead. The spirit of a person who dies in Christ, or "dies right," goes to rest and can help people; however, if an ungodly person dies, his spirit wanders about frightening and hurting people. 3) Obeah, the magic practiced by Black people throughout the West Indies, is the third realm of supernatural belief for people of Congo Town. When asked if they told their charges that people could hurt them, the caretakers generally responded that they did. The question was clearly related to obeah. One mother replied with the following: "I tell them about eating from anybody—don't press your luck—be particular what you eat. They can fix food and give it to you. They can work obesition and kill you. People could 'fix' clothes and shoes and things, too."

Of these three realms of supernatural belief, only the second one, the fear of spirits, was selected as an independent variable. The investigator determined that belief in God as an agent of help and punishment is virtually universal; variation comes only in the relative importance of helping and punishing and is slight. The third realm was not selected because the investigator was not able to identify an obeah practitioner in the community. It was therefore difficult to evaluate the fear of obeah.

Interviews were conducted to determine the method of punishment used as well as the number of situations responded to with punishment. The findings reveal that the most frequent punishment threatened and used in child-rearing in Congo Town is switching. The punitive instrument is most frequently a switch from a tamarind tree; it is long and supple so that it stings, but permanent injury cannot occur. All of the other measures of punishment cause some degree of psychological discomfort to the child: telling the child that God will punish him, sending the child to bed; warning the child about some other person, and so forth.

Otterbein was interested in the effect of this culturally shaped child-rearing system on the cosmology of the child. He suggested that projective techniques might indicate the extent to which these practices shape the attitudes of the children toward aggressive or malevolent supernatural beings. These practices may also influence the children's attitudes toward luck, predestination, achievement, and discipline.

Investigations of the belief systems shared by Black people of African heritage may provide information useful in classroom management, motivation, and possibly in instructional techniques for Black children.

Bridging the Gap: Afro-American Child-Rearing Values

The Black family has had to fulfill several functions because of the oppression it is called upon to mediate.

Preservation and Transmission of Racial Heritage

It has been the function of the Black family to celebrate the triumphs and heroes of the Black struggle and to remember the defeats.

Creation of an Alternative Frame of Reference

Wade Nobles (1974b) suggests that although the child-rearing practices in African-American families can be described in terms of African influences, they are also shaped by Black parents' conceptions of the realities they and their children face in America: white racism and economic oppression. The Black mother must prepare her child to "take on the appropriate sex and age roles (which by historical and philosophical definition are flexible, interchangeable and fluid) as well as the racial role (which by social and political definition are ones of resistance, suspicion and caution)" (p. 15).

Black child-rearing must resolve a basic conflict that exists between the European world view and the African world view. Nobles (1974b) describes these orientations as each possessing a "set of guiding principles, dominant values and customs and . . . behavioral and mental dispositions of a particular people." He describes the African ethos as being "survival of the tribe" and "oneness with nature." The cultural values associated with this world view are cooperation, interdependence, and collective responsibility. In contrast, the Euro-American ethos emphasizes the "survival of the fittest" and "control over nature." The cultural values associated with this world view are "competition," "individualism," and "independence." Dr. Nobles says that the role of the Black family has been to mediate these two opposing world views.

An interesting example highlights the role of Black women in reconciling opposing world views. As a girl scout I was taught service-oriented courtesies, such as helping the elderly across streets and giving up our bus seats to people who were our seniors. I recall being on a bus trip downtown with a girlfriend and her mother, who was our girl scout leader. We were seated together and hit upon the idea that we should give some white ladies our seats because they were our elders. My girlfriend's mother sharply reprimanded us and instructed us to sit in the next available seats and remain there, even though this was Columbus, Ohio, and we were not struggling over segregated buses. I am sure that the bus was symbolic of the struggle over segregated transportation in the South, and that struggle accounted for her strong reaction. However, the sharp distinction that this mother drew without explanation was that those girl-scout principles were nice, but they were not to be implemented in a situation wherein they conflicted with racial folkways and made it appear that we were deferring to white people.

Black parents have, in many cases, had to ignore white child-rearing norms irrelevant to the existential situation of their children. White teachers never cease to be amazed as they teach children not to fight (but to tell the teacher if someone hits them) when a Black child reports that his parents have told him to hit anybody back who hits him. The white teacher has no conception of the kind of reality a Black child has to face. Perhaps no one is around for him to tell, and a child must be able to defend himself from attack.

Duality of Socialization

A duality of socialization is required of Black people. Black children have to be prepared to imitate the "hip," "cool" behavior of the culture in which they live and at the same time take on those behaviors that are necessary to be upwardly mobile. Lawrence Levine (1977) has offered an explanation for the persistence of Black language in the face of the strong pressure to conform to standard English:

Living in the midst of a hostile and repressive white society, Black people found in language an important means of promoting and maintaining a sense of group unity and cohesion. Thus, while the appropriateness and usefulness

A duality of socialization is required for Black children.

of speaking Standard English in certain situations was understood, within the group, there were frequently pressures to speak the vernacular (p. 133).

Levine quotes a New Yorker who described the tension many Blacks perceived between peer group loyalty and the demands of the outside society.

When I was small and going to school, if you talked that way (Standard English), the kids would kid you, but we had a few kids that would do it, and we always kid them. . . . There was a girl who was always very proper . . . so, she'd always walk up and say, "Pardon, me." We'd all laugh; we knew it was correct, but we'd still laugh. Today, she end up successful (p. 153).

Levine describes further the problem of a dual language standard:

The lames [sic] might be laughed at within the group, but it was they who often had the better chance of mobility and success without. Black children hardly had mastered socialization to the behavior patterns and language patterns of their own group before they learned its disadvantages and low status in the larger culture.

Thus, for Black Americans, as for other minority groups in the society, the socialization process increasingly became a dual one: an attempt to live both within and outside the group (p. 153).

One of the challenges Black families must face in socializing their children is to understand and assist their children to function within their peer group. In addition, Black parents must also provide them with the skills and abilities they will need to succeed in the outside society.

Self-Concept Development

Black parents have been challenged to foster positive self-concept development in their children. They bolster their children's egos by such comments as "You're just as good as anybody else." They must soothe the anxieties that arise in their children when they engage in competition or social comparison with white children.

Socialization of Afro-American Males

Virginia Young (1970) has noted the early entry by Black children into the children's gang. Usually by the age of three a child must step down from "the throne" to either begin assisting with a younger child or to enter the group of older children. This process is more complete for male children; socialization into the peer group is accomplished at an earlier age. The male must become proficient in several areas. One is that he must learn to *walk*. Black people are a very rhythmic people and the way in which one moves expresses power or weakness through control of one's body. The special walk that Black males must master has been called "the pimp" or the "ditty bop." By the age of eight, a boy must create and perfect a distinctive way of moving his body. Even though he can use older boys in the community as models, he still must design a way of walking that is distinctively his own. This is called "getting your pimp together."

Another skill generally taught by the peer group (with supplementary help from fathers) is athletic prowess. Competitive sports are very important in Afro-American culture. Competency in sports is a manhood rite and is very important to one's status in the peer group.

Sexual competence is generally taught by the peer group. Most Black males begin sexual exploration by age ten and no later than thirteen. They are judged by their peer group on the basis of their success at seduction.

Another challenge for the Black male is to become *street-wise.* This "savvy" includes learning to fight. Most fighting instruction comes from within the family—from the father or older brothers. The peer group is the scene of practice for those skills imparted in the family.

A part of street-wise behavior is police avoidance. In research I conducted (Hale 1974) to determine the racial attitudes of Black preschool children, Black preschool males tended to associate white people with the police. When asked whether they liked white people, many of the males responded that they did not like white people because the police "like to fight," "like to kill people," "will put me in jail." One explanation for their attitudes may be the police-avoidance behavior male children learn from older peers on the street. However, not to be overlooked is that Black mothers and fathers have the keen awareness of policemen watching Black children more than they watch white children. Therefore, the socialization they give their children has had to include attitudes and strategies that enhance their survival in a hostile environment.

Black males are generally given early responsibility to earn income for special needs of their own (like buying a bicycle) or to contribute support to the family. Most boys by the age of eight have newspaper routes, grass to cut, or some other part-time job.

One of the challenges the Black male must face is the conflicting images of masculinity that predominate in the Afro-American community against the images that predominate in the broader society. This conflict grows out of the duality of socialization I mentioned earlier. However, it is particularly acute for Black males. The Black male between the ages of eight to fifteen is struggling to formulate an integrated conception of masculinity. The Afro-American culture projects a hip-walking, cool-talking model of masculinity. Dr. Ernie Smith of the University of California says that often Black males reject models of Black professional men because their behaviors and mannerisms are considered effeminate; they do not reflect the raunchy macho of the ghetto.* Dr. Smith also says that some boys feel they are flirting with homosexuality if they give in to the pressures of the school to exhibit behaviors they consider feminine.

An important manhood rite in the Black community is "playing the dozens." This is an activity primarily by males in which usually two opponents dual verbally. They make derogatory comments about each other and each other's family members (usually the mother). The performance of each player is appreciated and judged by the group who urges them on. This is called a manhood rite because it serves an important function. The boy must master several important competencies in order to be a good player. First of all, he must control his emotions. Here in the presence of his friends, terribly derogatory statements are made about his mother, who is dear to him. He must suppress his emotional reaction to what has been said so that he can think quickly and counter with an even more clever slur upon his opponent's mother. I contend that controlling one's emotions is a process emphasized in the socialization of Black males. Following are a few examples of dozens: "Your mother so old she got spider webs under her arms"; "You keep on talking 'til you make me think Your daddy was a bulldog, your mammy was a mink"; "You keep on talking 'til you make me mad. I'll tell you 'bout the troubles that your sister had"; "Your house is so small, the roaches have to walk sideways through the hallways" (Levine 1977, p. 352).

Socialization of Afro-American Females

Afro-American females have a very strong motherhood orientation, perhaps because girls are given early responsibility for the care of siblings. Girls are also usually given substantial household responsibility but are not expected to earn income outside the home. When girls have jobs, it is usually during adolescence, and they babysit or perform other domestic duties.

Facial beauty is deemphasized in the socialization of Black females because the standards of beauty set forth by the broader so-

---

*Comment made in a seminar at the annual meeting of the Black Child Development Institute in Houston, Texas, 1978.

ciety are based upon a white standard of beauty. Along with a deemphasis on facial beauty is a strong emphasis on personal uniqueness. Style is most important in the Black community. It is not only what you do, but *how* you do it. Tom Kochman has described an important difference in personality development in the Black and white communities. In the Black community one is admired for personal attributes rather than status or office. One is admired for verbal ability, personality, wit, strength, intelligence, speed, and so forth. As Black people have often held jobs that offered less power and prestige, they have acquired prestige within the group through the development of personal attributes. Kochman feels that the high valuation of the person, at least in part, is an adaptation to conditions of marginality and powerlessness. Consequently, Black females are not judged by white standards of beauty. A strong emphasis is placed on the development of sexuality, style, and personal distinctiveness. Not much attention is given to beauty potions and cosmetics, but considerable attention is paid to clothing and the rhythm with which she walks and dances. Femaleness in the Black culture is validated by the feedback she receives from boys regarding her sexuality.

Black females also consider bearing children as a validation of their femaleness. Consequently, a positive attitude is shown toward childbearing. This validation may provide an explanation for the disproportionate number of births by girls in their early teens.

A study was conducted by Diana Baumrind (1972) at the University of California, Berkeley. She identified several family patterns of Black and white preschool children and categorized the parents of Black girls as authoritarian-rejecting. The parents rated high on firm enforcement of rules. Black girls were expected to be more mature and conforming. The fathers did not promote non-conformity and were authoritarian. These socialization practices, she said, are authoritarian by white standards and would be regarded as change-worthy by many child-rearing experts. The findings of her study suggest the opposite—that the child-rearing practices characterizing Black families benefit their daughters.

Black females, she notes, in comparison with white females, appear to possess outstanding competencies. In this study the Black daughters of authoritarian parents were exceptionally independent and at ease in the novel, nursery-school setting. This observation is consistent with the observations of the researcher that many of the Black preschool girls carry considerable responsibility for the care of younger siblings at home; they play aggressively at nursery school; yet they sit quietly and attentively when they accompany their mothers to an evening nursery school meeting. By white standards, these young Black girls demonstrate unusual social maturity and a wide range of adaptive behavior. Baumrind suggests that something must be wrong with the pejorative connotation attributed to Black child-rearing practices. She suggests further that authoritarian child-rearing practices may have as their objective developing toughness and self-sufficiency in Black girls and that it is perceived by them not as rejecting but as nurturant caretaking.

Black females are imbued with a strong work orientation. Their socialization does not prepare them to expect a pampered existence as a housewife in a vine-covered cottage. Regardless of their social class, they are taught that they will probably be expected to contribute to the support of the family. Andrew Young once was questioned in a television interview about the fabulous houses Blacks in Atlanta own. He said they were indeed fabulous, but everyone in the houses was working to support them! One of the strengths of Black families identified by Robert Hill is that Black women can be counted on to contribute to the support of the family. This strong work orientation has its roots in early childhood socialization.

We need to investigate further the mother-child relationship among Black Americans. This research should have strong implications for educating Black children, particularly in early childhood settings. Greater continuity should exist between the behavior of the mother and the behavior of the teacher. One of the reasons white teachers have difficulty motivating and disciplining Black children is the cultural dissonance that occurs when the teachers behave differently from the way the children expect authority figures to behave. Black mothers tend to be more firm and physical in their discipline than white mothers. Consequently, when the child encounters a white teacher in school practicing all the techniques she learned in college, the children "run all over her" and are labeled discipline problems.

Another example of cultural dissonance may occur when Black children are placed in "open education" settings designed with white middle-class children in mind. As I pointed out earlier, many times Black children do not perform well when they are expected to learn independently, using educational hardware. They have the need for interaction with the teacher and other children because they are accustomed to learning through intense interpersonal interaction in the family.

Through careful study of the child-rearing of Black mothers and the resultant learning styles of Black children, we may obtain important information on how to achieve continuity between the home, school and community in educating our children.

Characteristics of Black Families that Influence Child-Rearing

Affective Orientation

The realm of feeling and affect and the cognitive processes arising from interpersonal relations may have important implications
for Black people. Research suggests that Black people are a very
emotional people. Some scholars have suggested that the emotion-
charged, people-oriented quality of Black expression is a part of an
African heritage:

*Knowledge in Western societies is largely derived from such propositions as
"I think, therefore, I am." The non-Western heritage of Afro-Americans suggests that knowledge stems from the proposition that, "I feel, therefore I think,
therefore I am" (Dixon and Foster 1971, p. 18).*

*The uniqueness of Black culture can be explained in that it is a culture whose
emphasis is on the nonverbal. . . . In Black culture, it is the experience that
counts, not what is said (Lester 1969, p. 87).*

This does not mean that Black people don't think or conceptualize their experience symbolically; rather, these scholars suggest that intellectual analysis disconnected from feelings leads to incomplete knowledge of the world (Haskins and Butts 1973).

Many research studies have found Black children to be more
feeling-oriented, people-oriented, and more proficient at nonverbal
communication than white children. We must determine the implications of this finding on their cognitive development (Gitter, Black
and Mostofsky 1972, pp. 63–78).

Brazelton (1971) compared infants born to Zambian mothers and
infants born to white American mothers. The health of the Zambian
mothers was not optimal. They had less protein in their diets because of its expense, increased infections, and more frequent preg-
nancies, which limited the recovery of the uterus after childbirth.
As can be expected, the Zambian infants weighed less, were shorter, and were less healthy than the white infants.

The two groups of infants were scored on days one, five, and ten
after birth. On the day one examination, the two groups were significantly different on six items. The Zambian infants scored lower
on following with eyes, motor activity, tempo at height, irritability,
rapidity of buildup, and alertness.

By day ten the Zambian babies had achieved greater advances
than the American infants. This improvement was attributed to the
affect implicit in the mother-child relationship.

Even though the African infants were not as healthy at birth, they
had surpassed the American infants in cuddliness, reactivity to
stimulation, alertness, social interest, and consolability. The

Zambian mothers provided a high-contact, loving environment for their babies. They were observed to have more handling and feeding contact with their infants than the American mothers.

Research (Young, 1970) has suggested that white children are object-oriented. That is, they have numerous opportunities to manipulate objects and discover properties and relationships. Consequently, this society's educational system is very object-oriented. Classrooms are filled with educational hardware and technology—books, listening stations, learning centers, televisions, programmed instruction, learning kits, and so forth.

Research with Black children, in contrast, has found them to be more people-oriented. Most Black children grow up in large families where they have a great deal of human interaction. I observed this high degree of human interaction while traveling in Africa. I was interested in the kinds of dolls with which the children of Ghana play. An African mother informed me that African children don't play with dolls, they play with their mother's babies! This high degree of people orientation may account for the indifference with which some Black children regard books and devices. This cultural trait may need to be acknowledged, and the result could be more human interaction in the learning process.

The work of Virginia Young (1970) is notable in its providing evidence about child-rearing practices that influence this "people orientation."

Even though household composition varies widely in the Black community, each is almost certain to contain many different types of people of all ages to hold and play with the baby. In many cases, the physical closeness between infants and adults is reinforced by the fact that they are often observed to sleep with their parents or either parent alone. There is a kind of rhythm found between eating and napping with short periods of each activity found with frequent repetition. This rhythm is very different from the disciplined long span of attention cultivated in middle-class child-rearing and expected in schools (p. 276).

Because the babies are held so much of the time, a direct response occurs to urination and bowel movements. Hence, from an early age, an association forms in the infant's mind between these functions and a response from the mother. Consequently, when the mother seeks to toilet train the child (in the early and stringent manner that has been observed in the Black community), the child is accustomed to her direct involvement in this process. In contrast, the transition is more startling for middle-class American infants whose functions have typically occurred alone. The mother begins to interfere with the bowel and bladder functions after many months of paying no attention to them (p. 278).

Young contrasts the highly personal interaction with the low object-orientation found in Black families. She noticed that few objects were given to the babies. The only type observed were some plastic toys that may have been picked up in the supermarket. Also, when babies reached to grasp an object or to feel a surface, they were often redirected to feeling the holder's face or engaged in a game of "rubbing faces" as a substitute. This inhibition of exploration is possible because "there are always eyes on the baby and idle hands to take away the forbidden objects and then distract the frustrated baby. The personal is thus often substituted for the impersonal" (pp. 279–80).

This affective orientation may be a critical factor overlooked in traditional educational settings. Rapport with the teacher in educational settings and rapport with the examiner in testing settings seems to be strongly related to academic performance for Black students and not very critical for whites. Zigler and his colleagues (Zigler and Butterfield 1968; Zigler, Abelson, and Seitz 1972) found that when a good rapport was established between an examiner during a standardized testing session, the Black children exhibited significantly superior test performance than when it was not. Such a difference was not found in the white middle-class sample.

Piestrup (1974) identified some factors that created good rapport in the teacher—Black student interaction, including warmth, verbal interplay during instruction, rhythmic style of speech, and distinctive intonation in speech patterns. When those factors were present, first-grade Black pupils showed increased reading proficiency.

Nonverbal Communication

It has been reported that a minimal amount of verbal exchange occurs in lower-class families. Young observes that this is because of the abundance of communication in other forms. She observed the people to look deeply into other's eyes, not speaking, but seeming to communicate fully. She suggests that parents use this means to impress a point on a child. Black people's avoidance of meeting the eyes of whites has been interpreted as a gesture of inequality. However, Young suggests that it may instead be a gesture of noncommunicativeness because of the extensive communication with the eyes within the Black group. Other forms of nonverbal communication are the mother's caressing the baby and children sitting in a circle rubbing bare feet. Young also notes what she calls a "mutuality" in family relations exhibited in remarks that pass between mothers and children:

"I'm tired," the three year-old girl complains. "I'm tired too," her mother responds. "I want some ice cream," the eight-year-old says wistfully as the ice cream truck passes. "I want some too," is the mother's way of saying no. This echoing of words and tone of voice is a common speech pattern. One does not see mothers and children clash and contend (p. 286).

Young concludes that distinctive cultural styles provide the milieu for the personality formation of Black children.

Out of this people-oriented, emotion-charged African heritage grows an ability to communicate extensively nonverbally as well as verbally. Some white educators had noticed that often Black children would not "look them in the eye" when they spoke to them. They considered this either to be a gesture of inequality or a sign of inattention. It may be neither. Two possible explanations exist for this. One is that it is a part of our African heritage to respect our elders. To look an authority figure directly in the eye is considered defiant and disrespectful. Another explanation is that Black people are very expressive nonverbally. Therefore, often the gaze of whites is avoided to cut off that intense level of communication that Black people share with each other.

Two studies (Newmeyer 1970; Gitter, Black, and Mostofsky 1972) provide support for the hypothesis that Black culture develops proficiency in nonverbal communication. Newmeyer had a group of Black and white boys act out a number of emotions nonverbally. The Black boys were better at enacting the emotions so that others perceived them correctly. Gitter, Black, and Mostofsky conducted a study with Black and white college students. Each student was tested by a member of his own race and was shown still photographs of professional actors taken while the actors were attempting to portray each of seven emotions: anger, happiness, disgust, sadness, pain, fear, and surprise. The subjects were asked to assign each of the photographs one of the seven emotions. The Black students made significantly more correct judgments of emotion.

Another example of nonverbal communication is found in the differences between the behavior of Black and white athletes in professional sports. During the 1977 basketball session when Kermit Washington of the Los Angeles Lakers critically injured Rudy Tomjanovich of the Houston Rockets, some people felt it was caused by a cultural difference in nonverbal communication. Rudy, who is white, said that he entered the fight area not to fight but to assist his teammate. However, Kermit, who is Black, interpreted the person charging toward him from the opposite team as a foe and

Many research studies have found Black children to be more feeling-oriented and people-oriented and more proficient at nonverbal communication than white children.

reacted spontaneously. It is interesting that none of the Black players charged into the area. In fact, Dr. J (Julius Erving) has been observed to *sit* under the bucket when a fight develops to communicate clearly that he is not involved. Kareem Abdul-Jabbar explained recently (*Jet* February 16, 1978) why most of his fights were with whites: "If you can buy this, it has to do with body language. Anyone from a Black community can obviously look at someone and say, 'I'm not going to fool around with this guy, because he's ready to fight.' A white player is slow to pick up on that."

Diane McIntyre* described this feeling-oriented spirituality that characterizes Black culture as it is expressed in the art of dance. She says that Black dance differs from white dance in that white dancers to a greater degree are into technical dancing.

The dancer makes a movement, not as an expression of feeling or as part of communicating an idea, but mainly to show that such a movement can be done. Black dance usually deals more with feelings and ideas. Don't get me wrong now. I don't mean to say Black dancers don't have great technique. There are Black dancers out there who can out-technique anyone, but this is usually combined with feeling and an emphasis on reaching out to communicate.

Diane McIntyre concludes that this difference is most likely associated with differences in Black and white culture. Art in Black society seems to have a spiritual role not evident in white art. However, that very quality often affects the ability of Black artists to become funded because funding is given on the basis of recognition. Most dance critics praise technique, evidencing little interest in emotions and communicating, but Black artists value these qualities as equally important. Therefore, many Black artists do not receive favorable reviews because their efforts are described as too simple and emotional.

An educational implication of this difference in nonverbal communication is shown in a study conducted by Byers and Byers (1972). They analyzed films of a white teacher interacting with two white and two Black girls of nursery school age. One of the girls of each race was very active in trying to get the teacher's attention with a noted difference in success. The white girl looked at the teacher fourteen times and was successful in catching the teacher's eye on eight of those occasions. The Black girl tried the same thing thirty-five times and was successful in four of those attempts. This difference could be the result of cultural differences in nonverbal communication. Analysis of the films showed that most of the Black girl's glances were at times when the teacher's attention was directed away from her so that she could not notice the attempt to get her attention through eye contact. The same was true in the affective area. The white girl seemed to sense when she could move

---

*Interview in *Essence Magazine*, September 1977, "Rapping with Diane McIntyre."

next to the teacher, sit on her lap, and so on, without disrupting the activity. The Black girl's attempts were timed differently, suggesting that she and the teacher did not share the same set of expectations and understanding of the meaning of gestures.

This difference in nonverbal communication should be investigated further because it may have implications for the kinds of rewards and punishments Black children elicit from the environment.

Physical Precocity and Movement

Numerous studies (Geber 1958, Ainsworth 1967, Brazelton, Koslowski, and Tronick 1971) have indicated that African infants are more developmentally advanced than European children during the first year after birth. This precocity has been observed at birth and has extended as long as three years; then it begins to level off and in some cases declines. Scientists are not certain whether the causes for this precocity are genetic or environmental. One explanation is that Black mothers handle their babies more and in a different manner than white mothers, and this handling stimulates accelerated development. A fertile area for research is to identify the causes for this precocity and determine strategies for extending it beyond the sensorimotor period into the cognitive realms of behavior.

Harry Morgan (1976, p. 133) suggests that Black infants are superior in all aspects of development when the mothers have adequate prenatal care. He also points out that Black children are motorically precocious. They are more active and have more physical energy to expend than white children. This physical precocity can be substantiated by the number of Black athletes who dominate major sports in numbers disproportionate to Black representation in the population.

Morgan maintains that the schools do not support the natural energy level of Black children. He suggests that Black children need an active environment for successful learning, particularly lower-income children whose parents emphasize survival skills rather than conformity, docility, and quiet manners—more typical of middle-class child-rearing.

Black children are described as entering school with excitement and enthusiasm, only to have the school crush their freedom and creativity. The children cannot channel their energy until given permission to release it. Consequently, many Black children elicit punishment and are labeled hyperactive because of their high motoric activity (p. 129).

Morgan believes that Black mothers often ignore their children's motoric precocity and do not seek to extend it because development in that area might interfere with the child's ability to be integrated into the school system of white low-motor expectations. This situation, he maintains, is detrimental to the natural learning styles of Black children. The school turns into a miniature battleground as it reacts punitively to the Black child's natural release of motor energy (p. 130).

Morgan suggests that Black children need schools that are "uncrowded, open, and airy with a great deal of natural light and plenty of private space for teachers and learners." He suggests further that model classrooms should be established for research purposes where "special nonpunitive environments are created as centers of learning for children who require more free space and movement than schools normally allow" (p. 130).

Some Black children, Morgan says, are able to quell their motor responses. Those who are not able to are usually in the lower-income levels and are labeled disruptive children, are prescribed medication, and are placed in "problem" classes where cognitive expectations are low; or they are suspended from school and ignored (p. 131).

Educators often complain that Black lower-income mothers do not provide enough toys for their children. Therefore, compensatory education programs purchase toys and playthings to distribute to them. Morgan indicts these efforts: "Little thought was given to the fact that the tinker-toy concept dictates that children are expected to sit in the crib or thereabouts and play quietly with their toys until their favorite TV program comes on. Without these toys, of course, mother and child touch, exchange various forms of communications and learn from one another" (p. 133).

In California in 1976, 25 percent of the children were classified as hyperactive. This group includes "approximately 2 million children who are taking tranquilizers, amphetamines, and Ritalin—the latter being a behavior-modifying drug." The effects of these drugs taken on a daily basis are not known. The only known fact is that the children are more quiet (Morgan p. 134).

The danger in these practices is that they force Black children to conform to a white cognitive model. They also make Black mothers more reluctant to support and extend the natural motoric responses of their children. When a mother constantly receives reports of misbehavior at school by older children, she may become more punitive and restrictive of the behavior of younger preschoolers. Morgan insists that "these mothers need encouragement and support in initiating and sustaining an active, thoughtful environment of unre-

Black children enter school with excitement and enthusiasm. But the school crushes the creativity from the children, who cannot channel their energy until given permission to release it.

stricted warm acceptance. Black children who find themselves too often among unwelcoming and uncaring adults and hostile institutions need all the developmental freedom they can muster to build muscle necessary for encountering the very white society in which we all live" (p. 134).

Wade Boykin (1978) suggests that the Black home environment provides an abundance of stimulation, intensity, and variation. A relatively high noise level exists with television playing a significant portion of the time and with constant stereophonic music playing. Usually, large numbers of people occupy a living space, and a variety of activities are taking place. This condition has been analyzed as "over stimulation" and as creating "conceptual deafness" by some social scientists (Maran and Lourie 1967, Goldman and Sanders 1969, Wach, Uygiris, and Hunt 1971). However, Boykin believes this Black, stimulating home environment produces greater psychological and behavioral "verve" in Black children than in white children in a middle-class setting. Exposure to more constant high and variable stimulation, he argues, has led to a higher chronic activation level. Therefore, Black children have an increased behavioral vibrancy and an increased psychological affinity for stimulus change and intensity.

It has been pointed out that schools are rather unstimulating and monotonous places to be (Silberman 1970, Holt 1964). Boykin suggests that factors like investigatory exploration, behavioral change, and novelty and variability have not been incorporated into the classroom. He suggests further that the reason white children are more successful at academic tasks than Black children is that they have a greater tolerance for monotony in academic-task presentation formats. They may not perform as well if they are faced with increasing levels of format variation and stimulation or if they were asked to utilize movement more in the learning process. On the other hand, perhaps Black children are not as successful in school because they are relatively more intolerant of monotonous, boring tasks and the sterile, unstimulating school environment.

Boykin describes "verve" as having a behavioral and a psychological dimension. As an example of behavioral verve, Boykin suggests that Black children may learn faster with techniques that incorporate body movement into the learning process. Guttentag (1972; Guttentag and Ross, 1972) found that Black preschool children possess a greater movement repertoire than both lower and middle-class white preschoolers. She has also shown that Black children learn simple verbal concepts easier when they utilize movement than when they are taught by a more traditional format. On the other side of the coin, Massari, Hayweiser, and Meyer (1969) have found that the children who can inhibit movement have higher IQ scores. Boykin is presently investigating the effect of incorporating movement into educational settings because of the academic performance of Black children.

By psychological verve, Boykin means that variation or stimulation in task formats may make a difference in improving the performance of Black children. Rohwer and Harris (1975) found that fourth grade Black children learned prose more easily when it was presented in a variety of formats (oral, written, or by pictures) as compared with presenting it in only one way. No difference was evident when a combination of media was used with white children. Piestrup (1974) found that the most effective teachers of reading for first-grade Black children were those who varied their vocal intonation and engaged in rhythmic verbal interplay with the children. This is compatible with the observation by Virginia Young that a "contest" style of speech exists between Black mothers and children in which they volley rhythmically, and the child is encouraged to be assertive and to develop an individual style. Young also suggests that Black mothers give directions for household tasks in a distinctive manner, approximating the call and response patterns found in Black music. (A mother's communication of directions in household tasks uses few words, and tasks for which she has to give instructions are broken down into small units with brief directions for each following short task.) The effectiveness of the use of rhythm in speech and verbal interplay by teachers of Black children may connect culturally with Black children who interact rhythmically with their mothers at home.

Boykin has found in his own research (1977) that varying the format in problem solving presented to Black and white children did not make a difference in the performance of the white children, but the Black children performed markedly better with the varied format.

Boykin concludes that affective stimulation and vervistic stimulation are necessary for the Black child to be motivated to achieve in an academic setting. Without this stimulation Black children become turned off and seek other arenas for achievement and expression. He suggests that "perhaps we can facilitate the academic/task performance of the Black child if we increase the "soulfulness" of the academic task setting.

Black Conversational Style, Speech, and Reading

Speech and the Black Migrant Child

Laura Lein (1975) conducted a study of the speech behavior and linguistic styles of Black migrant children. She found an emphasis upon spontaneity and general participation. In the home, conversations in migrant camps are occasionally slow moving but are almost always open to general participation. "Children talk with adults, play verbal games with them, and argue with them, although usually in joking terms. Speech interaction at school often involves long monologues with limited participation by others" (p. 3).

Even in church emphasis is placed upon spontaneity and general participation, with call and response between the preacher and the congregation. Verbal interchanges such as "Amen," "Take your time," "Tell the story," are not regarded as interruptions but as encouragement. In fact, the minister will elicit such verbal evidence of attention and support by cajoling the congregation, "You don't want to hear about that," to which the congregation will respond that he should "tell it like it is." An individual often spontaneously begins a song or extends a song and gives a testimony during the service. Lein points up the contrast in the classroom atmosphere:

At work, at church, and at home, success is valued by migrants, but competitive success is not as important as general participation. The church, the extended family organization of the migrant camp, and the family organization of the work crew all emphasize cooperation rather than competition.

Children who go to school from migrant camps are faced with important contradictions between home and school. The traditional classroom does not emphasize the qualities of spontaneity, participation, and independence from adults which mark children of migrant camps. Many activities in school are not open to general and spontaneous participation. For instance, teacher monologues or presentations to the class are not meant to be interrupted (p. 3).

The first category Lein calculated was speech frequency. She observed thirteen migrant children in four settings: at home with parents present; at home with adults absent; at school, supervised by the teacher and at school unsupervised by the teacher. She found that migrant children speak less in the supervised classroom than in any other setting. In the classroom they speak considerably less than do students considered able by the teachers. A difference exists also between the home and the school in what Lein calls symmetry, that is, the extent to which both speakers talk equally. Teachers in the classroom speak much more frequently than does

At school, students are expected to remain in their seats, moving about only at the direction of their teachers.

anyone in any of the other settings. Migrant parents in the home speak only a little more than do the children in their presence. Migrant children speak most in groups of peers in settings where everyone talks approximately equally.

Lein's second category was speech complexity. In analyzing one student's speech, she found that the complexity varies from setting to setting. In discussions with peers, a student was most organized. He used complex sentences, provided elaborate evidence in support of his statements, and spoke to the point. At home with his brothers and sisters, he paid close attention to argument and responded appropriately. With his parents present, his speech was more compressed, possibly because they were all watching television. However, he still used a number of complex sentences. In contrast, his speech in the supervised classroom was almost monosyllabic, when he spoke at all.

Lein's general findings regarding speech complexity are that the children speak their longest utterances among their siblings and cousins when they are unsupervised by adults. They use their simplest speech for the classroom in the presence of teachers. They are more prone to use complex language in the presence of parents than teachers. In general, in the settings where migrant children speak the least, they speak most simply.

Lein suggested some reasons for the quantity and quality of migrant children's participation in the classroom. One reason is fear of misinterpreting speech. She suggests that the interaction between white teachers and Black students, particularly Black adolescents, in public school classrooms is peculiar in many ways. One of these is that teachers, in the position of authority in the classroom frequently fear their students. When teachers are afraid, they may misinterpret statements in a way that reinforces their fear. Lein observed that the migrant children tease parents and older relatives and engage them in playful argument, but there are few attempts at verbal combat or pressure. Teachers relatively unacquainted with this stylistic game-playing react as if the children were seriously challenging their authority.

To understand how the school is structured to prevent children from participating, Lein contrasted the behavior expected at church with the behavior expected at school. The church was selected because it was a setting in which similar demands are made on the children but to which they respond differently. The church services are lengthy (three to four hours) but almost all migrant children behave well in church by the standards of parents and other church members.

However, there are at least two differences between appropriate behavior at church and at school. At school, except in the kindergarten and first grade, students are expected to remain in their seats, moving about the room only at the direction of their teachers. Such sanctioned movements are relatively infrequent. In church, children are expected to spend most of their time in their seats, but the movements demanded by participating in the church service involve frequent standing and walking around. As a church service proceeds, people who "have the spirit" shout and move around the room. In addition to this scheduled movement, it is acceptable behavior for children to get up at will to go to the bathroom, to change seats, and to quiet and fondle children younger than themselves. . . . Both more regulated, scheduled movement and more spontaneous movement are acceptable in church than in the school classroom (p. 10).

Lein also notes the contrast in the freedom to verbalize at church and at school. At church a number of scheduled events occur for verbal participation by the congregation such as singing, responsive reading, testimonies, voting to accept new members, and so forth. In addition, as noted before, extensive call and response continues between the congregation and the speakers. "This is in contrast to the classroom where attention is more usually marked by silence or by questions and remarks at relatively long intervals. Acceptable indicators of attention and appropriate participation by the child are different in school and in church. And the prerogatives of the children are different" (p. 10).

Lein observed that migrant children usually display their speech skills only in settings in which they speak with some regularity. She suggests that at school, participation and skill demonstration are frequently silent activities. "Eye contact rather than verbal contribution is a sign of attention and participation. Demonstrations of ability are usually in the form of individual trials of new skills before the teacher" (p. 10).

This study points out a number of incompatibilities between the culture of the school and the culture of the home. Lein concludes that teachers need to listen to students speak in contexts that exhibit their best speech skills.

Demanding examples of good speech from students in tests or in the usual classroom situations is not necessarily an effective way of finding out what students know. Listening to exchanges between peers and peer evaluations of such exchanges is an important part of discovering how children speak. Also, it is a reasonable mechanism for learning how children interpret and react to speech. Teaching teachers the skills of anthropological observation and analysis may be one helpful way of enlarging their understanding of what is happening in the classroom (p. 10).

Sarah Michaels (1980) conducted an ethnographical study of sharing time in an urban first-grade classroom with one-half Black and one-half white children. She emphasizes that the oral discourse skills of children are important precursors to their literary skills. She found a significant difference between the oral-presentation styles of the Black and the white children. The white children utilized a style that she calls topic-centered. This style was compatible with the teacher's notion of a good sharing episode. The discourse of these white upper middle-class children tended to be tightly organized and centering on a single topic or series of closely related topics.

In contrast to the topic-centered style, the lower-income Black children, and particularly the Black girls, were far more likely to use what Michaels calls a "topic-chaining" style—loosely structured talk that moves fluidly from topic to topic, dealing primarily with accounts of personal relations. The teacher experienced difficulty following the theme of the stories because she expected the narrative to focus on a single topic. These sharing turns gave the impression of having no beginning, middle, or end and hence no point at all. The result was that the Black children seemed to "ramble on" about a series of commonplace occurrences.

With the white children who used a topic-centered style, the teacher was highly successful at picking up on the child's topic and expanding on it through her questions and comments. Her questions generally stimulated more elaborated focused talk on the same topic.

With many of the Black children, on the other hand, the teacher seemed to have difficulty identifying the topic and understanding where the talk was going. Therefore, her questions were often mistimed, stopping the child in the middle of a thought. Also, her questions were often inappropriate and seemed to throw the child off balance, interrupting his or her train of thought.

The teacher made several attempts to "teach" the children to select and stick with one topic. However, these attempts were confusing to the children. Her first strategy was to state that appropriate topics for sharing were events that were "really, really very important and sort of different." However, the children still had difficulty with this notion.

Later in the year the teacher tried emphasizing a new sharing principle, which was that the children should tell about only one thing. However, the Black children still encountered difficulty in conforming to the topic-centered style.

Michaels noted that this narrative style is the same one identified in informal home conversations between selected children and their mothers as well as in conversations among peers outside the classroom. This observation supports previous research that suggests a conversational style that is a feature of Black culture.

Additionally, Michaels observed a Black instructional aide in the classroom who led sharing time on one occasion. Even though the aide was in general a less skilled teacher of reading and math than the regular teacher, during the sharing session she led she was better able to pick up on the children's narrative intentions, ask them appropriate questions, and help them round out and organize their narrative accounts.

The problems the teacher had with the Black children seemed to stem from a cultural mismatch between the teacher and child. Such mismatches over a period of time resulted in the white children having more of an opportunity to participate in sharing time, receiving more practice, and feeling better about their oral exchanges with the teacher. Inasmuch as sharing time develops skills that are useful when children begin to write topic-centered prose, this ethnic-group disparity in discourse style could lead to serious educational problems.

Ann Piestrup (1974) conducted a study wherein she identified six techniques of first-grade reading instruction that were utilized with children who speak a Black dialect. She found that the children had the highest proficiency when they were taught with the "Black Artful" approach. These children were taught by a Black teacher who was comfortable using the dialect with the children. She also spoke rhythmically, varied her intonation, and engaged in verbal interplay with the children. This teacher combined a high degree of verbal rapport with high involvement in the lesson.

This study is compatible with the observation by Virginia Young (1970) who described a "contest" style of speech between Black mothers and children, in which they volley rhythmically and the child is encouraged to be assertive and to develop an individual style.

Teachers who use rhythm in speech and engage in verbal interplay with Black children may connect culturally with those who interact rhythmically with their mothers at home.

The research of Donald Henderson and Alfonzo Washington (1975) is an example of investigation of Afro-American cultural patterns that may have implications for educational practices. They first affirm that Black children are culturally different from white children. This difference can be directly attributed to the fact that Black children mature in communities that are culturally different from the communities of the broader society.

The experiences through which the Black child develops his sense of self, his social orientation, and his world view are provided by institutions (such as family, religion) whose characters, structures and functions are very often unique to the Black community. The school, on the other hand, reflects the culture of the wider society and is often unaccommodative to the culturally different Black youngsters. Indeed, often these differences are defined as deficiencies. These deficiencies are assumed to be significant impediments to "proper" learning in school. Therefore, massive attempts at remediation are undertaken (often, to the detriment of the child). In effect, many school practices are inappropriate for treating the educational needs of Black youngsters. An appropriate treatment of the educational needs of Black youngsters must take into account their unique cultural attributes (p. 353).

Henderson and Washington examine the processes of social control in the Black community and contrast them with the practices of an elementary school in which one of the authors worked. They suggest that adults in the Black community play substantially different roles as social control agents than do adults in the school. They indicate that a network of significant adults firmly corrects undesirable behavior whenever it occurs and report such behavior to the parent. Therefore, parents are at the center of this social control network. For the child, this means that he is always under the surveillance of adults. The significant feature of the control system is that it seems to operate external to the child. Therefore, the child seems to develop external locus of control.

In the school situation, adults seem to behave as if locus of social control exists within the child. They do not function in ways that are consistent with the child's expectations of how adults should behave toward them in situations that require the enforcement of social controls. Henderson and Washington also discovered that the parents and the teachers almost never communicated. Few of the parents participated in the school's P.T.A. program, and none of the teachers lived in the community in which most of the children lived. "In short, the social control apparatus of the school functioned in a way that was quite different from that of the community and did not immediately include the parents in its operation" (p. 358).

Based upon interviews with forty-six Black adults, the investigators came to two conclusions that may explain the "uncontrollable" behavior of many Black youngsters in the school.

1. The young child learns (probably very quickly because he has older children to help him) that adults in the school do not function in the same way that adults do in his community and that only behavior of gross impropriety (flunking, suspension) will be

reported to his parents because school adults are not community agents of social control. He is free to act "like he wouldn't act at home."

2. The lore of "school readiness" suggests that children come to school socialized in such a fashion that the locus of social control has been internalized. Hence, teachers expect Black children to behave as "good" children should (and good little white children do). It seems that the children and the teachers have mutually incompatible expectations of each other. Over a period of time, they tend to work out rather shaky adjustments to each other. The teachers conclude that the children are incorrigible, and the children conclude that the teachers are inconsistent and capricious (p. 358).

The researchers observe that many behavioral problems of Black children can be ameliorated by modifying the social control system of the school. They suggest that each parent replace the principal at the center of the school's social control apparatus for their own children. Teachers and principals should behave as do significant adults in the community. In short, a need exists for further research into the social control system employed in the Black community and for its introduction into the school.

Hope J. Leichter (1973, p. 244) moves this discussion closer to the classroom and the community in her development of the concept of educative style. Although the ideas that are related to learning style are important for the development of the concept of educative style, the concept of educative style is broader in that it addresses learning itself, but it also addresses the "ways in which an individual engages in, moves through, and combines a variety of educative experiences." She uses the term *educative style* to include school and nonschool institutions, claiming that the "cultural distance" in educational values between parents and teachers should be explored. She asks to what extent the school reinforces, complements, contradicts, or inhibits the efforts of the family and community, and to what extent the family and community reinforce, complement, contradict, or inhibit the efforts of the school. In her opinion, children learn from many "significant others" as well as from school teachers. Educators should gain an understanding of how a person moves through and utilizes diverse educative experiences over a lifetime (p. 239).

Leichter also has some interesting suggestions for the method of studying educative style. She recommends observation as well as obtaining data from numerous natural settings that are the bases for day-to-day events.

*This is consistent with a basic presumption that it is essential to understand
the significance of that which appears to be trivial, particularly when the trivial recurs. . . . Therefore, research on educative style requires that the investigator have the ability to shift, not only from one time perspective to another, but also from one scale of behavior to another (p. 246).*

She suggests, further, that biographical data may be useful, as
will the study of social networks. This information would permit
the tracing and analyzing of an individual's interaction with the
"significant others" in his life. It would describe the lifespace of the
individual and would examine the way he or she moves from one
educative experience to another in different settings (p. 247).

Leichter warns against the current trend of determining educational policy by considering single variables and treating aspects of
education in isolation. The concept of educative style looks at the
total social (cultural) situation of the individual. Much confusion
has resulted in the educational arena from disjointed considerations
of the influences of the culture on education. For example, at one
extreme, policymakers in early childhood education advocate re-
moving the lower-class child from the home and providing compensatory experiences; others advocate subsidizing the mothers to
remain at home with their children instead of working. Some of the
extremes of this kind of debate could be averted if some theoretical
perspective could postulate the best combination of family, community, and school effort. Leichter observes that "in designing programs and considering questions of the most effective points for
educational intervention, the issue of how individuals combine
educative experiences and the styles by which they educate *themselves* both in early childhood and later in life is clearly fundamental" (p. 249).

Four

Play Behavior As an Indicator of Cognitive Style

Give That Gal Some Cake

The first day I played in the sand, the
* sand got in my eye;*
The second day I played in the sand,
* the sand made me cry.*
I went over to my Grandma's house,
* and asked her for some cake.*

She turned me 'round and 'round,
* and 'round, and said,*
"Give that po' gal some cake!
Oh, give that gal some cake; oh, give
* that gal some cake!"*
She turned me 'round and 'round
* and 'round, and said*
"Give that po' gal some cake!"

—a folk song

Psychology and early childhood education have given serious attention recently to child's play because it is a natural intellectual activity; a child, in effect, teaches herself through play, spontaneously exploring objects, either in a solitary manner or in varying degrees of interaction with other children and adults.

The study of child-rearing practices by Black families is crucial to identifying the manner in which Afro-American culture shapes the behavior of Black children. It is equally significant that through play the culture is expressed or celebrated. The study of child-rearing is an examination of what "goes in." The study of play behavior is the study of what "comes out."

Research into the play behavior of children in general has been extensive, but research into the play behavior of Black children has been limited. An examination of the existing studies reveals a pre-

Play is the natural intellectual activity of the child. One's culture shapes one's play behavior.

occupation with comparing the play styles of Black and white children and with teaching Black children certain play styles thought to affect significantly important learning variables. The overriding orientation is to access a play style and then correlate the behavior with a score on a standardized assessment instrument. Although some scholars of play have suggested that one's culture shapes one's play, few if any scholars have conducted ethnographical studies of the play of Black children to determine the manner in which the Black milieu shapes the play behavior and the expressive styles of Black children. If it is true that one's culture shapes one's cognition, research in early childhood should specifically describe that process. Play behavior may be a fertile area of investigation. An examination of a few exemplary studies in this area clearly establishes the need for new direction in the research of Black children's play.

T. V. Busse (1970) conducted a study to determine whether enriching the Head Start classroom environment with play materials would affect the social development of Black preschool children. The Preschool Observation Schedule was used to assess social interaction differences between experimental and control classes. The most clear-cut finding concerning social development was that the boys in the experimental classes engaged in more cooperative play with toys than did the control boys. No difference existed in the types of play behavior between experimental and control girls. The conclusion was that social development of boys, but not girls, can be helped by the enrichment of play materials.

Borowitz, Costello, and Hirsch (1972) attempted to assess the effect of play on four-year-old Black children. *Effectance* was defined as a child's independent effective interaction with his world of people and things. They developed two scales. The first scale defined organization, involvement, and interpersonal responsiveness in play; and the second operationally defined the psychosexual content of play. The categories in these instruments may be useful. However, because the researchers are psychiatrists, a strong emphasis upon Freudian interpretations of play behavior exists.

Paula Eder's study (1972) was concerned with discovering whether Black children exhibited deferential behavioral patterns toward white children when they were placed in an interracial dyadic play group. The study demonstrated that the Black subjects deferred to the white subjects. The author advocated a strong and more extensive development of Black power and Black identity in the schools to counteract this tendency.

Vivian Anderson (1975) conducted a study designed to determine whether the sociodramatic play behavior of Black and white children would be similar when socioeconomic status was held constant. The subjects were fifty-four Black and fifty-four white kindergarten children of high socioeconomic status. Each group of four subjects (two boys and two girls) were studied for one thirty-minute period in a special playroom. Each child's mental ability was measured immediately after the play period by the Goodenough Drawing Test. Black subjects engaged in sociodramatic play scored significantly better than the whites, but no significant relationship was found between IQ scores and the level of sociodramatic play.

Catherine E. Rosen (1974) conducted a study to determine whether the development of skill in sociodramatic play would enhance the problem-solving behavior among Black lower-income children. Four kindergarten classes serving Black lower-income children were the subjects of this study. Two classes were given forty days of instruction and practice in sociodramatic play. Compared with two control classes, the experimental group showed significant improvement in three areas: post-test group problem-solving behavior, effectiveness in solving group problems requiring maximum cooperation and maximum competition, and role-taking skills. These results support the prediction that acquisition and performance of sociodramatic play improves the problem-solving behavior of Black lower-income children. Rosen used a standardized observation schedule to rate the complexity of play.

The foregoing review reflects the previously reported orientation of research concerning the play behavior of Black children. It also reflects the fragmentation and lack of systematic investigation that can lead toward theory development. Despite the paucity of research in this area, experts in the field share my opinion that research into the play of Black children should be fruitful.

Brian Sutton-Smith (1972) agrees that play is culturally determined and that its effects vary among ethnic groups. Nancy Curry (1971, p. 61) reports that at the symposium on play sponsored by the National Association for the Education of Young Children (NAEYC), the participants raised the question of whether play themes were universal or whether one sees different play themes in differing sociocultural backgrounds.

In an earlier article, Sutton-Smith (1967, pp. 360–70) postulated that play serves multiple functions in child development. Often psychologists place exclusive emphasis on contributions to a child's emotional development and social learning, but Sutton-Smith asserts that play serves an important function in the development of cognitive abilities.

Over the years, psychological testing has been the preferred technique for assessing the individual educational needs and abilities of children. Although such tests are valuable in some circumstances, a major criticism of their use with Black children has been their cultural bias. Another problem has been the almost exclusive focus on cognitive skills rather than on accessibility for learning (Meier 1964). These tests also have limited value with preschool and kindergarten children. For adequate assessment of educational needs and strengths, it is necessary to consider not only the level of the child's cognitive skills but also his emotional development.

Studying the play of a child offers an opportunity to assess both aspects of his functioning. According to Borowitz (1970, p. 216), play is the natural "work" of children and the symbolic expression of their personalities. "Surprisingly," he states, "little effort has been directed toward measuring those specific aspects of play behavior which could provide clues to the young child's level of competence."

From an educational perspective, a child's play is believed to reflect the degree to which she can impose her own sense of structure and sequence on the external environment; it also reflects not only the degree to which her perceptual and cognitive structures have been developed but also the extent to which they have been integrated and can be applied to new situations. Therefore, play can be regarded as an index to the level of the preschool child's overall cognitive competence.

Well established in the literature is that a child's play has significance for her intellectual growth. Piaget believes that play permits a child to make an intellectual response in fantasy when she cannot make one in reality and thus protects her sense of autonomy. In addition, it helps consolidate learnings acquired elsewhere and prevents them from dropping into disuse. Brian Sutton-Smith believes that play serves important functions in the child's emotional development and in social and cognitive learning. Bruno Bettleheim (1971, p. 34) describes play, as, "a means of making possible things that might not have been possible in reality."

It is important that adults take play as seriously as the child takes it.

A distinct difference exists between play and games. Play allows a child to express her inner feelings, to escape to a world where she is in command of some situations or to escape from a game that she may be losing, when losing may be a little more than she can bear at that time. A game, on the other hand, imposes rules and regulations to which the child must adhere, and it leaves little room for personal expression. Play is not always an unhappy experience or an escape mechanism. Sometimes it can be the continuous repeating of a pleasant experience that occurred in reality that brought happiness to the child, who wants to continue to experience the feeling. Since play, whether autonomous or under adult supervision, is important for the development of the child, it is important that adults take "play" as seriously as the child takes it.

Millie Almy (1967, p. 274) suggests a need for further investigation of a child's cognitive activity during spontaneous play. The available theory and research clearly support the idea that spontaneous play can contribute significantly to a young child's developing intelligence. Almy urges observation of children's play to see how it is organized and categorized.

What attributes or properties do the children notice as they encounter objects and materials? How effectively do they label these and other experiences? What kinds of relationships enter into their awareness? What kinds of reasoning are revealed in their play? Do they proceed from one particular instance to another particular instance, picking up some similar elements or are they beginning to weigh situations deductively? What kinds of inferences and generalizations do they make? What sorts of contradictions do they notice? To what extent do they see situations from only their own point of view, and to what extent do they stand, as it were, in another's place? (p. 275.)

Almy (p. 276) further notes that this task demands, "keen awareness of each child, what he does and how he thinks today, as well as where he was yesterday and where he may go tomorrow."

Most studies of child's play are interested in some aspect of the following dimensions: time for play, place for play, things for play, and people for play. The study of Black children's play should consider those features. But beyond that, this book's study of Black children's behavior goes beyond the present focus of play research. A comprehensive ethnographical analysis of the self-directed behavior of Black children in their home environment must precede a cognitive analysis of play. We must first conceptualize the cultural context of Black children's behavior before we can extract meaning from the behavior. The present philosophy of social science and its

We must first conceptualize the cultural context of Black children's behavior before we can extract meaning from the behavior.

understanding of the Black cultural milieu make impossible an attempt to analyze the cognitive styles of Black children engaged in any type of behavior.

We must even broaden our conception of play to encompass Black children's *expressive styles* that include a range of behavior, tastes, and preferences that we might not ordinarily include as a part of *play behavior*. Some of the modes discussed below may appear to be only peripherally related to play. However, we must guard against "common sense" knowledge and conduct a wide-ranging examination of at-home interaction that can provide descriptive information about the world view of the Black child.

Movement

Movement is an examination of the amount of space utilized during play and the manner in which that space is utilized. It might be significant to determine the amount of time the child spends in quiet activities as compared with active movement. This determination might have implications for the length of time adults should require children to sit and concentrate on tasks. My cursory observations

Black children, especially active in their home environments, are penalized as hyperactive in the school.

suggest that Black children (particularly males) are very active in their home environments, and as a consequence they are penalized as hyperactive in the schools.

Dance

What are the stages by which Black children respond to music? How much encouragement are they given as toddlers to walk and to dance? Could early expressions of rhythm through dance have any influence upon the physical precocity of Black children that has often been observed and reported? Does early proficiency in dance affect mathematical ability in terms of early proficiency in utilizing and locating the self in space?

Music

What are the stages by which Black children respond to music? How prevalent is music in the Black environment? What is their preferred type of music? How often are songs sung to children and by children? What songs are sung? Why are Black children remarkably able to memorize popular songs? How can that ability be utilized in other types of learning?

Environmental Arts

A need exists to study Black home environments. Most descriptions of Black home environments have focused upon deprivation as defined by white America. A description of the environment in which Black children live, play, and develop should encompass artistic descriptors as well as analyses of indicators of affluence and educational enrichment. Note should be taken of color preferences in furnishings in Black homes as well as any other distinctive features in decor, furniture styles, and arrangement. This information may be useful in designing learning environments for Black children. What if, for example, it were discovered that Black children learned most effectively or exhibited distinctive moods based upon the colors that were used on the walls of the classroom?

Fashion Arts

It has long been accepted that Black people emphasize personal distinctiveness in their dress. Black males in particular have impacted the fashion industry and set many trends, among them wide-leg pants as well as bright colors in men's suits and shirts. Studying types of clothing worn by Black children for various occasions could prove significant. This study would note the choice of colors, fabrics, and styles and would compare clothing worn at home and clothing worn at school. Significant also might be the extent to which children are dressed according to the tastes of their parents and at what age they begin to express preferences and make choices. Those choices could be analyzed to determine the extent to which they are shaped by the Black cultural milieu. Fashion is a very important cultural vehicle for expressing creativity.

Folklore

An ethnographical study of expressive styles should record the folklore of Black children. Most studies of the language of Black children are interested in language from a linguistic perspective, that is, the structure of its usage. However, it might also be useful to study the verbal skills of Black children, including such expressions as "rappin'," "shuckin'," and "jivin' "; "running it down," "coppin' a plea," "signifyin' an' soundin'." There are also stylistic dimensions of the oral tradition in Black culture as described by Smitherman (1973): call and response, rhythmic pattern, spontaneity, and concreteness.

In considering folklore, an ethnographical study should be conducted of games, stories, chants, jump-rope rhymes, and curse words. After these cultural artifacts are recorded, they can be analyzed to ascertain the psychological processes they reflect.

Another aspect of play behavior might be affected by the folklore of the Black community. An understanding of Black folklore would facilitate the interpretation of fantasy among Black children. Fantasy is important in the development of children. The ability to fantasize is very closely related to the development of creative thought and cognitive ability. However, understanding the way in which the culture of the Black community affects the fantasy of Black children is important.

Nutrition

A popular slogan says, "What you eat is what you are." If that is true, study of the nutritional environment of Black children could be important in interpreting their behavior. The study of Black foods should encompass food selection, preparation, and spicing. Definite trends in these areas are common to Black people and are related to the African heritage. This information would have obvious implications for health services, and it would be helpful in

What you eat is what you are.

planning nutritional curricula for Black school children. Many day-care and child-development programs design their menus from nutrition manuals with little thought to the nutritional preferences of children that have been shaped by their culture. Many of the meals prepared in institutional settings are rejected by the children. This may be another area in which school is defined by the child as a strange, alien environment.

Joyce Rookwood* of the Administration of Children, Youth, and Families/HEW suggests investigating the feeding patterns of Black families. This information could be useful to programs like Head Start. Presently, teachers are instructed to utilize "family style" feeding in which the children are seated in groups and conversation is encouraged. Ms. Rookwood first questions the definition of "family style"—whose family? She observed a teacher in a Head Start center who was having the children eat one by one. She questioned the teacher about the practice. The teacher replied that this pattern of eating was more similar to the style of eating of many of the children at home wherein family members "catch a plate" whenever they arrive and are hungry. She found that these children played less at the table, ate more, and seemed to feel better, possibly from better digestion. The teacher observed that the children eat better when they can concentrate on *eating* rather than telling the teacher the color of the peas.

Magico-Spiritual Beliefs

The spiritual mode of the Black child should be studied as an expression of his cosmology. Investigators have noted a deep concern with the spiritual and the supernatural in the creative activities of Black children, who have been observed to express interest in ghosts and religious rituals.** Examining these modes will help teachers to understand better the cosmology or world view of the Black child and to determine the implications for concept development.

Many theories and hypotheses have developed about play, one of which is the equating of play with "transcendence." Play may have the ingredients to allow us to transcend and, for a moment, remythologize life. Recent authors have given play the status of theology, indicating that play contains elements also found in religion. This

*Comment offered during a seminar I conducted at the annual meeting of the National Association for the Education of Young Children (NAEYC) in New York City, August 1978.

**Personal conversation with Michele Rubin, Director of Arts-in-Education at Clark College, Atlanta, Georgia, 1975.

philosophy is called "new play." For Neale, play is peace; it has the connotation of meaningfulness; it involves delight. In his book *God and Games,* Miller (1969) views play as a response to the introduction of the sacred into our lives. Jurgen Mültmann (1971) calls for transcendence of the win-loss nature of much of our play so that we can simply be who we are in and through play. For Harvey Cox (1969), festivity is a way humans keep alive to time by relating past, present, and future; play has a festive element.

Transcendence is often linked with religious or mythical systems wherein gods and deities exist beyond human time. Concepts such as fantasy, daydreaming, and imagining are closely linked to transcendence and occasionally allow human beings to get beyond reality and existence. The "peak experience" of Maslow (1968) is a super perceptual state—a form of sensual opening that can become the vehicle for transcendence.

Five

The Humanities
As a Source of
Black Culture

You've taken my blues and gone—
You sing 'em on Broadway
And you sing 'em in Hollywood Bowl,
And you mixed 'em up with symphonies
And you fixed 'em
So they don't sound like me.
Yes, you done taken my blues and gone.

You also took my spirituals and gone.
You put me in Macbeth and Carmen Jones
And all kinds of Swing Mikados
And in everything but what's about me—
But someday somebody'll
Stand up and talk about me,
And write about me—
And sing about me,
And put on plays about me!
I reckon it'll be
Me myself!

Yes, it'll be me.

—Langston Hughes*

These words of Langston Hughes capture the concern of Afro-Americans for the preservation, projection, and celebration of Black

Note: Grateful acknowledgment is made of the contributions to this chapter of Professors Edmund Gordon, Vincent Franklin, and (the late) Charles Davis of Yale University.

*From *Selected Poems of Langston Hughes*. Reprinted by permission of Alfred A. Knopf.

101

culture as it is expressed in the creative arts. Even though white folklorists, artists, and scholars were the collectors, performers, and interpreters of Black culture, in the early history of the African experience in America, Black creative artists emerged earlier than Black social scientists to articulate Black culture. Surges in Black consciousness were felt, such as the Harlem Renaissance in the 1920s—an explosion of Black creative expression.

The civil rights movement gave birth to the modern surge of Black consciousness in the 1960s. Many "Negroes" converted to "Black." From the street corner to the university, intense dialogue began about issues like liberation, struggle, Pan-Africanism and cultural nationalism. Political theorists of the '60s began to affirm a view associated with the 1920s that the preservation and interpretation of Black culture is as essential to the liberation struggle as political and economic reform.

Courses in Black studies were demanded by students and teachers in universities across the country, and alternative schools were created for younger children. These schools were concerned with ideology, culture, and values, and with defining and implementing a "Black education."

However, transforming the settings and curricula of schools that educate Black children to include the literature, history, music, and philosophy of the Black world is only one aspect of the needed transformation. Also important is realizing that Black children may be experiencing severe learning disabilities because of differences between the culture in which they develop and learn and the culture they encounter in most public schools.

Psychologist Wade Boykin (1978) has suggested that a kind of "soulfulness" characterizes Black culture. Black people create distinctive cultural forms when they interact with language, music, religion, art, dance, problem solving, sports, writing, and other areas of expression. The task before us is to conceptualize this "soulfulness" of Black culture and demonstrate its relationship to the present difficulties many Black children face in adjusting to "traditional" academic settings.

Traditional Schooling

A debate is now going on in the American educational community over the effectiveness of the public school system in socializing and training Afro-American children. Some educators argue that the school system has been effective in replicating the social system generation after generation, decade after decade, allowing those individuals to succeed who accept the values generated by the dominant Euro-American culture and inculcated by the schools. Thus, the high failure and dropout rates among black and other minority students is considered the intended consequence of school systems developed to reproduce the social class structure of twentieth-century capitalist America. On the other hand, other educators and community leaders suggest that America is an open, competitive society and that individuals of different cultural backgrounds can advance themselves through the public schools. One reason for the high failure rates of some cultural minorities is the mismatch between the school culture and the social, cultural, and experiential background of minority children. Thus, an improvement in the school performance of Afro-American and other culturally different children in the public schools will occur if the school curriculum and environment are changed and made to reflect more closely the particular learning styles and cultural background of the students.

Social scientists present other explanations to explain the high rate of failure among Afro-American children in the public schools. The Black home environment has been labeled "pathological," and Black parents have been accused of failing to prepare their children adequately for school. But if the cultural orientation of the Afro-American home and community is different from that of the public schools, educators need to understand this orientation and its relation to the school performance of Black children.

Toward a New Foundation for Black Education

A new approach to the education of Afro-American children is needed. Black parents generally want their children to master the tools of mainstream society so that they can be economically viable and can contribute to the creative development of their community and society. At the same time, the Black community wants to preserve and celebrate aspects of Afro-American culture. At times the expressive styles of Black children, often resistant to change, may be the cause of tension between teachers and Black children in educational settings. These culturally specific expressive styles may be related to academic failure, increased disciplinary problems, placing Black children in low-expectation academic tracks, and the early termination of academic careers. The results of these conditions are familiar statistics on Black teenage unemployment and imprisonment.

It is imperative that educators conceptualize these expressive styles that emerge from Black culture so that an educational model can be developed to serve a two-fold function. First, this model will imbue Black children with the competencies they need to survive and to be creative in America. Second, it will change the way Black children are perceived and treated in the educational process. Instead of bombarding Black children with a white cultural/cognitive model as in the past, educators will use this new model as a way of facilitating the educational process of Black children in American schools.

The Proposed Study

From what source shall we create the foundation for such a model? A coherent data base to draw upon for creating this model does not presently exist. This base must be multidisciplinary at least.

A group of social scientists are now contributing to a growing body of psychological information on Black culture, child-rearing, and cognition (Boykin 1978, Simmons, 1979, Hale 1980a and 1981, and others). However, the vast majority of studies in the social sciences often reflect an Anglo-American or at least a Euro-American bias.

A source of information that Black social scientists have been overlooking is found in the humanities. This discipline contains rich data about Black culture precisely because the creative artists were expressive long before a significant number of Black social scientists began to produce research. An analysis of the cultural artifacts of Afro-Americans may provide us with information about the meanings of Black culture (as it relates to socialization) from the viewpoint of the participants in that culture. Such a study would provide an expanded understanding of Black culture through an analytical perspective that bridges the humanities and the social sciences.

An effort of this type would not only be beneficial to Black psychology, it would also be useful to the social sciences and the humanities. The twentieth century has seen considerable progress in the social sciences concerning the mechanisms of human growth and development. Contemporary social scientists can tell us a great deal about the interaction between human and environmental characteristics that account for behaviors. However, they have not matched the humanities in their understanding of what life means. The social sciences deal with the *mechanisms* of human development, and the humanities deal with the *meanings* of human development.

The social sciences can be advanced if they utilize the meanings provided by the humanities. The humanities can be advanced by the influence of the structure, precision, and consensus validation of the social sciences. And they can do this without the loss of values derived from the subjective tradition of humanistic endeavors. Both categories would gain from such a bridge.

This chapter addresses the subject of creating a methodology that can enable psychologists to extract data from the creative arts and utilize them to extend our research efforts.

Following is a study that has been designed by a group of scholars at Yale as a beginning effort to struggle with design and methodological issues. The study was initially funded by the A. Whitney Griswold Humanities Research Fund at Yale University with a grant to the late Professor Charles Davis and to me. This proposal represents months of dialogue and struggle by a multidisciplinary group of scholars to operationalize an idea into a bona fide (if avant-garde) research study. Though the study is incomplete, we share it at this stage to stimulate other research projects of this type and possibly to add legitimacy to this kind of research in the fields of early childhood education and developmental psychology (which are oriented toward experimental, empirical research). Even though Black scholars must eventually connect with the mainstream and produce quality empirical research, we still must do the necessary work to lay the foundation for our research in order to infuse the disciplines with our viewpoint.

Design of the Study and Methodological Issues

This study is an examination of Afro-American music, art, and literature for reflections of the urban, northern, working class, contemporary Black experience (conceptualized as roughly encompassing the period between 1950 and 1980).* This period was selected because previous works, notably Lawrence Levine's *Black Culture and Black Consciousness* (1977) and Thomas Webber's *Deep Like The Rivers* (1978), have analyzed music and literature that reflect the (southern) slavery and (southern/northern) post slavery/pre-World War II period).

Design issues were raised that are germane to each discipline. However, an overall issue was one of selecting the genres so that comparability was possible across the disciplines. For example, we were in danger of comparing a folk expression in art, such as fashion, with fine art, such as painting. Therefore, we decided to stratify

---

*The study design and methodology represents the collective thinking of Dwight Andrews, doctoral student in music; Sylvia Boone, assistant professor of Afro-American studies and art history; Vincent Franklin, assistant professor of Afro-American studies and psychology; Janice Hale, research associate in psychology and lecturer in Afro-American studies; and Caroline Jackson, graduate student in Afro-American studies and literature—all of Yale University.

the genres in each discipline so that the various strata, from folk culture to fine art, would be represented in each discipline. Therefore, storytelling in literature; popular music in music (rhythm and blues, gospel, disco, rapping); and fashion arts, Christmas cards, and poster reproductions in art would represent folk culture. Novels, autobiographies, and short stories in literature; Black art music in music; and painting and sculpture in art would represent the fine-art strata of culture.

In the following sections, each discipline is discussed in terms of design and methodological considerations.

Literature

Two major approaches to conducting the literary study were considered. One approach was to examine literature for devices that could be compared to music and art that can yield information about Afro-American culture. An example would be repetition, rhythm, circularity, tone, and so forth. The other approach was to examine the works for the themes that arise and the information that can be gleaned about Black socialization. For our initial investigation, we decided upon the latter approach because of the paucity of prior research to guide the former investigation.

We are utilizing the aforementioned works of social scientists to compare their hypotheses and findings about Black life to the themes that arise from creative writers.

We chose the following genres. The number beside each indicates how many should be analyzed to yield a representative subset of the estimated universe of works:

novels (15) short stories (25)
autobiographies (10) storytelling/humor
plays (5) (recordings) (5)

In order to select the works to be analyzed, we will compile a list of literature that treats the late twentieth century, urban, northern Black experience. We selected a group of Black literary critics to poll for choosing the works to be analyzed.

Music

In trying to identify Afro-American cultural values in musical expression, we had to consider the important issue of the criteria for selecting a work. We felt that since music is popularly consumed, we could select music on the basis of record sales to Black people. We discovered that the figures on record sales of Black artists are both inaccurate and difficult to obtain.* Further, it is even more difficult to distinguish among artists who owe their popularity solely to Black buyers, because the most financially successful artists are those whose sales are inflated by the white "crossover" market (for example, Earth, Wind, and Fire; Stevie Wonder; Diana Ross; Donna Summer; The Jackson Five; and so forth).

Louie Robinson suggested that the judgment of our panel concerning what artists and songs are popular among Blacks is as valid as any figures we could obtain from the record industry (this advice was based upon his attempts to obtain this information for his magazine article on this topic).

We decided also that content was as important as popularity. Popularity enters in because these are the songs that have been produced and disseminated to the Black community via the recording industry. However, from that group we are selecting those that in our judgment are the most salient to the concerns of our study: those songs most reflective of the Afro-American world view and most instructive of values that contribute to socialization. Songs are being identified from the following categories: Black art songs, gospel, rhythm and blues, disco, and rapping.

Even though the focus of the study will be upon the song lyrics, we acknowledge that the analysis of the music will have to take into consideration the intricate interaction between the text (lyrics) and the structure of the music. Because of our sensitivity to this interaction, we will seek to include (but not limit our selection to) as many writer/composer/performing artists as possible. Because it may be difficult to untangle the web of lyric writer, musical composer, and performer, we will be sensitive to focusing upon those works that are examples of the combination (for example, the songs of Earth, Wind and Fire, Stevie Wonder, Chic, Curtis Mayfield, Ashford and Simpson, Marvin Gaye, and many others).

Art

We will examine also narrative representational art works. We have identified several forms that exemplify the cultural as well as the artistic realms. The following art forms will be analyzed: painting, sculpture, fashion arts (hairstyles—hats, clothing), Christmas cards, posters, and popular reproductions.

To simplify the selection process for painting and sculpture, we selected two artist groups that are avant-garde ideologists: Africobra Group (Jeff Donaldson) in Washington, D.C., and Weusi Artists in

---

*Personal conversation with Louie Robinson, author of "Top Black Record Sellers of All Time" in *Ebony Magazine*, February, 1980.

New York City. They were selected because they create art that projects an alternative image of Afro-Americans, defined by Sylvia Boone as "What we are and what we see ourselves as."

For the cultural realm of fashion arts, Christmas cards, posters, and popular reproductions, we will analyze collections of slides, photographs, newspaper clippings, advertisements, mail order catalogues, and magazine pictures of Afro-Americans.

An additional feature will be added to the study of this discipline because of the nature of art and the state of the science of art history. Interviews with contemporary artists often provide us with the opportunity to gain additional insight into the artists and their work. Art is different from literature and music in that it does not "speak for itself." And though there are those who argue to the contrary, at least we can assert that the voice is not always clear. Therefore, we propose to conduct interviews of artists to obtain information about the validity of our hypotheses and thus supplement our own analyses of Afro-American artistic expression.

Interviews are an important component of this phase of the study because of the state of the science of art history. An examination of texts on Afro-American art and artists (Fine 1973, Lewis 1978) reveals a focus on biographical information on the artists, but very little analysis of the artifacts. Our study will make a contribution to this area by providing a more scholarly analysis of the message of Afro-American art.

Critique of Two Examples

We admit that the type of research we have described is groundbreaking. In our review we found only two examples—one in literature and one in music—that assist us in clarifying the approach of our study.

The first study is entitled: "She Who Is Black and Mother" (Wade-Gayles 1980). This study is exemplary because it seeks to "draw an in-depth portrait of the Black mother in America as she is presented in selected novels and in selected sociological studies . . . highlighting three features: 1) child-rearing posture, 2) maternal aspirations, and 3) maternal fulfillment" (p. 90).

The goals of Wade-Gayles's study are laudable. Unfortunately, her analysis bogs down. The first problem is her selection of the works. Five of the novels were written over four decades. They all place the Black mother at the center of the development of plot and theme. Wade-Gayles states that all have received critical attention in reputable journals. It seems to be a good idea to select novels that span the entire period being studied, and to select those that give attention to the Black mother. But a third criterion (of critical acclaim) seems much too broad and nebulous as a selection crite-rion because the author is not specific about the definition. Are these the only novels about the Black mother to receive "critical ac-claim," as she defines it, during this period?

We raise these selection questions because Wade-Gayles sum-marizes each novel individually but does not shed much light on the three dimensions of the study outlined. Since she has selected only five novels, we can assume that she is not trying to represent Black life with the few characters in the novels. Moreover, she does not attempt to pull the depictions of the five women into a coherent statement; unfortunately, they are left dangling.

It is a much easier task to identify the major sociological works (because there are so few). Even though Wade-Gayles's field is lit-erature, she does a fine job of critiquing the sociological works. However, when she begins to contrast them with the fictional works, she digresses into contrasting the amount of attention each discipline gives to each topic instead of extracting useful informa-tion about the depiction of Black mothers.

Ultimately, Wade-Gayles tells us more about the usefulness of conducting a study of this type than she tells us about what we can learn about the Black woman and about child-rearing from the works she has examined. Though a step in the right direction, the major shortcomings of the study are inherent in its design and the selection of the works to be analyzed.

The second example is entitled: "Perspectives on Black Families from Contemporary Soul Music: The Case of Millie Jackson" (Stewart 1980). In this paper, Stewart reviews the sociological liter-ature indicating a paucity of Black males to serve as desirable mates and heads of households to Black females and Black families. He describes a phenomenon that has evolved that he calls "sharing," that is, a marriage triangle of a man, a wife, and a mistress. Of in-terest is that Joseph Scott (1976) has conducted a sociological study in which he interviewed wives and mistresses to chart the dynamics of this relationship. Stewart compares Scott's findings with his anal-ysis of two albums by popular rhythm and blues recording artist Millie Jackson, who has produced two "concept" albums that deal explicitly with this "sharing" relationship.

Stewart at times provides contrasts between Scott's interview data and Jackson's lyrics, but more frequently demonstrates how the two data sources complement each other.

Stewart's brilliantly executed study demonstrates the validity of Millie Jackson's lyrics as a source of data by pointing to the impor-tant parallels in Scott's interviews. Additionally, Stewart reveals the unique evidence Jackson's insights offer that supplement the "existing empirical evidence and suggests a number of questions that further analytical research might pursue" (p. 67).

Stewart demonstrates effectively the value of a study such as his that utilizes the humanities to inform the social sciences: "The analysis of Millie Jackson's treatment of the sharing phenomenon undertaken above clearly shows that the capacity to articulate complex insights about social phenomena is not limited to scientists" (p. 70).

Stewart's work is exemplary because he effectively selected works from sociology and the creative arts that treated the same phenomenon. Then he gleaned useful information, argued effectively for the validity of this line of inquiry, and offered a specific example. Stewart suggests that some aspects of Black culture can be lost "by limiting the techniques of analysis and presentation to standard procedures which require translation into 'objective observational language.' " He suggests further that the "mix of cognitive modes employed by Millie Jackson would be closer to that of the Black masses than that employed by a social scientist. This means that data obtained from folk culture media will display a certain uniqueness and can provide a cross check on the validity of analytical data" (p. 71).

Our proposed study will be difficult but exciting. The search for a methodology to uncover the essence of the Black experience is not new, but thus far little systematic research has been done. We thus view this proposal as the "next step" in the struggle for understanding, echoing DuBois (1957):

When in this world we seek truth about what men have thought and felt and done, we face insuperable difficulties. We seldom can see enough human action at first hand to interpret it properly. We can never know current personal thought and emotion with sufficient understanding rightly to weigh its causes and effect. . . . There is but one way to meet this clouding of facts and that is by the use of imagination where documented material and personal experience are lacking (p. 316).

Six

Afro-American Roots: Interviews With Grandmothers

Mother to Son

Well, son, I'll tell you:
Life for me ain't been no crystal stair.
It's had tacks in it,
And splinters,
And boards torn up,
And places with no carpet on the floor—
Bare.
But all the time
I'se been a-climbin' On,
And reachin' landin's,
And turnin' corners,
And sometimes goin' in the dark
Where there ain't been no light.
So, boy, don't turn back.
Don't you set down on the steps
'Cause you finds it kinder hard.
Don't you fall now—
For I'se still goin', honey.
I'se still climbin',
And life for me ain't been no
    crystal stair.

—Langston Hughes*

A central hypothesis of this book is that certain characteristics peculiar to Black culture have their roots in West Africa and have

Note: Grateful acknowledgment is made of the collaboration of Professor Sandra Scarr (Department of Psychology, Yale University) in the conceptualization, design, and data analysis in this chapter.

*From *Selected Poems of Langston Hughes.* Reprinted by permission of Alfred A. Knopf.

implications for the way Black children learn and think. As a part of exploring the issue of the participation of Afro-Americans in a distinct culture, we have examined in the preceding chapters evidence that the African heritage survived the American slavery experience and described the mechanisms of retention and transmission of that culture. Our research is a beginning effort to describe the influence of Afro-American culture on socialization in general and child-rearing in particular.

I conducted interviews with Afro-American and Euro-American grandmothers in order to identify values and practices that have been transmitted generationally. Disciplines of the social sciences, literary, and folkloric sources were drawn upon to formulate hypotheses that are thought to represent an Afro-centric or Anglo-centric ethos. Hopefully, the clusters of values will advance the effort to reinterpret differences that are thought to exist in the behaviors of Black and white children. Even though these differences are apparent, they are often pejoratively defined. Conceptualizing the behavioral patterns and learning styles of Afro-American children in a cultural example will enable us to complement rather than oppose Afro-American culture in the educational process.

Background of the Study

During the summer of 1978, I made my initial investigation into the child-rearing practices of Black grandmothers in the Sea Islands (Edisto and St. Helena) and in Charleston, South Carolina. My research was supported by the Laboratory of Comparative Human Cognition of Rockefeller University (under the auspices of Michael Cole and William Hall). I selected the Sea Islands area because it is reported to be a fertile area in the United States for identifying an Afro-centric value and behavioral system.

I interviewed thirteen Black women. Their socio-economic status ranged from lower-income to upper-middle-class. The interviews were tape-recorded and consisted of open-ended questions. I compiled approximately 100 questions salient to Afro-American child-rearing and child-rearing in general. Each interview lasted from between 1½ to 2½ hours.

Transcribed, these interviews formed the foundation for the development of the instrument of the study. I discarded and reworded many items. Long answers provided a frame of reference for conceptualizing a southern Afro-centric perspective.

Herskovits (1958) suggests that two streams of Afro-culture are rich with African retentions. One emanates from Dahomey (Africa) to Haiti (Caribbean) to Louisiana-Mississippi (USA). He describes a type of magic (voodoo) that provides the foundation for medical practices and religious beliefs. The other stream emanates from Ghana (Africa) to Jamaica (Caribbean) to South Carolina-Georgia (USA). A type of magic (hoodoo) is distinctive to that area of the country. Even though he identifies the two streams, Herskovits suggests that the most fertile area for identifying African retentions is in the Sea Islands of South Carolina and Georgia.

Method

Instrument

The instrument was a precoded interview form that consisted of approximately 183 items and six checklists. The questions were organized into files that reflected the hypotheses of the study. The hypotheses grew out of prior conceptualizations by the investigators from examining the literature of psychology and Afro-American studies. The files were as follows:

1. Human orientation vs. object orientation
2. Physical activity
   feeding
   toileting
   movement
3. Social breadth
4. Religious orientation
5. Achievement orientation
6. Variability of home environment
7. Autonomy/Discipline
8. Willfulness/Assertiveness/Style Aggression/
   Confrontation Independence/Obedience
9. Adaptability of Family roles: child care tasks/housekeeping tasks
10. Creative Arts
    music/dance/tv
    fashion arts
    visual arts
11. Food Preference
12. Attitudes toward abortion/conception

In addition to the questions of the study, extensive background information was obtained on the respondents and their families. The significant results are reported below in the description of the subjects.

The interviews were conducted in a place designated by the respondents, usually in the home or in a room in the Senior Citizen's Center. The interviews were between 1½ and 2½ hours in length.

The responses were recorded on the interview form and tape recorded. The thirty interviews were all conducted by the same investigator, who is an Afro-American female.

Subjects

The subjects of this study were thirty Afro-American and Euro-American women who had all reared at least one child. The subjects ranged in age from fifty-five to eighty-five years with a mean age of seventy-two for both groups. They were all grandmothers.

The subjects were contacted through three Senior Citizen's Centers in New Haven and North Haven, Connecticut.

An attempt was made to sample the values of women who represented the dominant Anglo-Saxon Protestant orientation of American society.

Subjects who were of northern and eastern European origin were identified by the directors of the Senior Citizen's Center. These women were approached individually and asked to participate in the study.

Table 5 presents the ethnic origins of the Black and white grandmothers and their husbands.

Table 5

Ethnic Origins of Black and White
Grandmothers and Their Husbands

Race	Origin	Grandmothers		Husbands	
		No.	%	No.	%
Black	Afro-American	15	100	14	93.33
	Caribbean	0	0	1	6.67
White	English	3	20.00	1	7.14
	Scandinavian	2	13.33	2	14.29
	French	2	13.33	1	7.14
	German	3	20.00	4	28.57
	Irish	2	13.33	4	7.14
	East European	2	13.33	4	28.57
	Canadian	1	6.67	1	7.14

The t-test* procedure was utilized to determine whether a difference existed between the number of people living in the Black

*A test of significance is used to determine whether the differences between the means of the scores of the two groups of subjects is significantly different or whether the difference is due to chance. It also indicates how probable it is that the differences we have found between our samples will also be found in the populations from which they are drawn.

One selects the type of test of significance based upon the characteristics of the data. The t-test makes three assumptions about the scores obtained in causal comparative research. The first assumption is that scores form an interval or ratio scale of measurement. The second is that scores in the populations under study are normally distributed. The third is that score variances for the populations under study are equal (Borg and Gall 1971, p. 304).

households and the number living in the white households of these grandmothers. No significant difference was found, but previous studies have indicated more reliance upon the extended family among Blacks than among whites. To determine whether this was true, a chi-square* distribution was obtained on the proximity of the grandchildren to their parents and grandmothers. No significant difference was found between the proximity of the Black and the white grandchildren to their parents. However, a difference existed between the proximity of the Black and the white children to their mothers (the respondents of the study). The Black children lived closer to their mothers. The Black grandchildren lived significantly closer to their grandmothers than the white grandchildren. The fact that the Black grandmothers live in closer proximity to their children and grandchildren than the white grandmothers implies the possibility of greater mutual reliance, although no tendency existed for them to live in the same household.

The chi-square distribution of the proximity of the child to the grandmother is summarized in Table 6.

Table 6

Proximity of Child to Grandmother

Proximity	Black		White	
	No.	%	No.	%
Same city and state	114	80.00	44	51.00
Same state	11	7.80	15	17.65
Same region	15	10.64	3	3.53
Outside region	1	.71	23	27.06

p<.0001

The study found a tendency for Black senior citizens to be economically active after the retirement age. Dorothy Harper, director of the Senior Citizen's Center from which the Black subjects were drawn, stated that the Black seniors were not as available to participate in the center's activities because they could not afford to be "retired." They had to do odd jobs and domestic work that would provide additional income but that would not interfere with their

---

*Chi-square is a nonparametric statistical test often used in causal comparative studies, particularly when the research data are in the form of frequency counts. These frequency counts can be placed into two or more categories. A chi-square test can be computed from this frequency data, and the resulting chi-square value tells the researcher whether the distribution of frequencies differs significantly between the two groups (Borg and Gall 1971, pp. 312-13).

social security. Additionally, many of the women were still involved in child-rearing. Some of them were rearing grandchildren, providing live-in care for great-grandchildren, or engaging in extensive babysitting.

No significant difference existed in the marital status of the two groups of women. Both groups were either married or widowed in similar proportions (an interesting finding in light of research that suggests a high divorce/desertion rate in Black families).

Significant differences were discovered in the areas in which the Black and the white grandmothers were born and spent their childhoods. This information is useful for tracing the geographic roots of any cultural orientations in the data.

From the Afro-American grandmothers we were particularly interested in determining the number who had roots in the southeastern United States. Herskovits (1958), as we have mentioned, suggests that the core of Afro-American culture (rich with African retentions) is found in the Sea Islands of South Carolina and Georgia. A qualitative analysis of the responses (particularly about folklore) indicated that the southern-born and reared grandmothers were more Afro-centric. The chi-square distributions for areas of birth and childhood are summarized in Tables 7 and 8.

Table 7

Area of Birth
(Grandmothers)

	Black				White			
	Grandmothers		Husbands		Grandmothers		Husbands	
Area of Birth	No.	%	No.	%	No.	%	No.	%
Europe					3	20.00	1	6.67
Northwest U.S.					1	6.67	1	6.67
Northeast U.S.	8	53.33	1	6.67	9	60.00	13	86.67
Canada					2	13.33		
Southeast U.S.	7	46.67	13	86.67				
Caribbean			1	6.67				

The t-test was used to analyze the occupational prestige of the grandmothers and their husbands. The occupational prestige was rated with the Duncan and NORC* scales. The difference in the

---

*The Duncan and NORC are two separate scales for rating occupational prestige. Each occupation is ranked for its relative prestige and given a score. A t-test was used to determine where a statistical difference existed between the means of the two racial groups.

Table 8

Area of Childhood
(Grandmothers)

| | Black | | | | White | | | |
| | Grandmothers | | Husbands | | Grandmothers | | Husbands | |
Area of Childhood	No.	%	No.	%	No.	%	No.	%
Europe					1	6.25	1	6.67
Northwest U.S.					1	6.25	1	6.67
Northeast U.S.	9	60	1	6.67	13	81.25	13	86.67
Canada					1	6.25		
Southeast U.S.	6	40	13	86.67				
Caribbean			1	6.67				

Grandmothers p<.01
Husbands   p<.001

prestige of the occupations of the grandmothers on the Duncan was significant at the .003 level* and on the NORC at the .005 level. The overall difference was significant at the .04 level, the white grandmothers having the most prestige.

The prestige of the occupations of the husbands was significant at the .004 level on the Duncan and not significant on the NORC. The overall prestige of occupation of husbands was significant at the .04 level in favor of the white husbands.

These differences were interesting because the subjects were drawn from a working-class population. *Working class* was defined as skilled or semiskilled workers and as secondary school graduates or less. Significant differences between the white and Black groups existed within that category.

No significant difference existed between the educational levels of the grandmothers. However, a significant difference was found in the overall prestige of the occupations of males and females and in the prestige of occupations of Blacks and whites overall, summarized in Tables 9 and 10.

---

*The t distribution is used to determine a significance level. If the difference between the means is significant at the .05 level, that is, there is one chance in 20 (.05) that this large or a larger difference would occur if there were in fact no difference between population means. Most researchers will reject the null hypothesis (or accept the experimental hypothesis) if the t is significant at the .05 level. Occasionally the more stringent .01 level is chosen. At this level there is only one chance in a hundred that the researcher will reject the null hypothesis when, in fact, it is correct. The rejection of the null hypothesis when it is correct is called a Type I error. Obviously if we lower the significance level required to reject the null hypothesis, we reduce the likelihood of a Type I error. At the same time, we increase the likelihood of a Type II error, that is, the acceptance of the null hypothesis ("no difference") when there is in fact a difference (Borg and Gall 1971, p. 287).

Table 9
Prestige of Occupations
by Sex

Sex	Number of Subjects	Prestige Score Average
Females	222	247.37
Males	189	298.037

p< .01

Table 10
Prestige of Occupation
by Race

Race	Number of Subjects	Prestige Score Average
White	156	345.20
Black	255	225.07

p< .001

An interesting mobility pattern emerged from the prestige-by-generation-by-race analysis. White families showed a slight increase in prestige of occupation from the first to the second generation and a sharp decline in prestige in the third generation. In the Black families, even though the prestige level is significantly below that of the white families, an increase in the prestige of the occupation was found in each generation. The third-generation Blacks have almost reached the level of the whites.

Mobility Pattern: Generation by Race

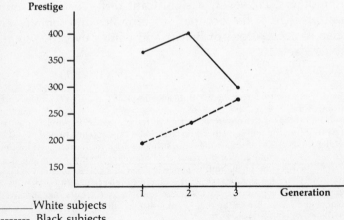

_____ White subjects
---------- Black subjects

Child Background Information

No significant difference existed in the number of children of the Black and the white grandmothers. However, the Black grandmothers had significantly more grandchildren and great-grandchildren than the white grandmothers. An analysis of the distribution of the children and grandchildren's ages revealed that the Black women gave birth to their children at an earlier age. Fifteen Black grandchildren are in the age range of thirty-two to forty, compared with zero children in that age range among whites. In other words, a shorter generation length exists among Blacks.

We found no significant differences in the areas of birth for the Black and the white children of the grandmothers. However, significant differences existed in the areas in which they spent their childhoods. The chi-square distribution for the children's areas of childhood is summarized in Table 11.

Table 11

Area of Childhood
(Children)

Area of Childhood	Black		White	
	No.	%	No.	%
Midwest			2	2.11
Far West			3	3.16
Northeast	144	87.80	89	93.68
Northwest	1	.61		
Southeast	19	11.59		
Other			1	1.05

We found a significant difference in the educational levels of the Black and the white children. However, no significant difference existed in the educational level of the Black and the white grandchildren. This finding reflects an upward mobility among the Blacks.

The chi-square distribution for the children's educational level is summarized in Table 12.

Results

The results of the study will be discussed in two parts. The first will be a discussion of the files that reflected a significant difference when all of the items were summed and analyzed by a t-test procedure. The second part will be a discussion of the files that were nonsignificant when summed. Mention will be made of items within the file that were significant.

Table 12

Educational Level of Grandmothers' Children

Level of Education Completed	Blacks		Whites	
	No.	%	No.	%
Less than 8th grade	12	7.32		
8–11th grade	65	40.25	15	16.29
12th grade–3rd yr. college	73	44.51	71	77.17
College grad	9	5.49	4	4.35
More than college	4	2.44	1	1.09

p<.0001

Part 1
Human Orientation vs. Object Orientation

The sixteen questions in this file were intended to determine the extent to which the grandmothers valued physical contact, responsiveness, use of gadgets, toys, and equipment with young children.

Items one through three and six through seven were developed, based on a film, *Cradle of Humanity,* produced by UNICEF. It depicts African child-rearing in documentary fashion. The African mothers were shown giving distinctive massages to their infants. The narrator explained that the parts of the body were massaged symbolically for their function. Also, a powdery mixture was used for the massage.

The narrator of the film reported that European women often handled their babies delicately, as if they would break. He pointed out the contrast in the vigorous way the African mothers handled their babies. This behavior may be a clue to the reported physical precocity of African (and Afro-American) babies. The following questions were planned to determine whether massaging and shaping a baby physically is pervasive among Afro-Americans and unknown to Euro-Americans. The difference indicated by the data suggests that this may be an African survival.

The following is a listing of the questions and their significance level. All of these items were in a positive direction for the Black respondents:

(1) Is there any special way in which you should rub or massage a baby? Black—yes (p<.0001).
(2) Is there any particular oil, powder, or mixture you use to massage her? Black—yes (p<.0001).
(3) Do you talk to the baby when you massage him? Black—yes (p<.0001).

(6) Are there things you know about that a mother can do to make a baby look a certain way? (Shaping the head, nose, hair.) Black—yes (p< .005).

(7) Which of the following have you heard of:
   a. Shaping a baby's nose by massaging it so that it will be pointed? Black—yes (p< .0001).
   b. Shaping a baby's head? Black—yes (p< .0004).
   d. Shaping a baby's legs and feet? (This item was provided by the grandmothers.) Black—yes (p< .03).

The four choices in item 7 were added and analyzed. Item 7c was included even though it was nonsignificant: applying baby oil to a baby's hair so that it will be straight. The difference in the sum of the items was significant (p< .0001), positive for the Black respondents.

Two items were positive in the white direction that were contrary to the hypothesis. The white subjects reported a nearly significant tendency to be more responsive to a crying baby:

(4) How often should you respond to a baby when she or he cries?
   a. never   c. when she wants to be held
   b. occasionally   d. as often as possible

This tendency of the Black grandmothers to be less responsive (item 4) and to hold the babies less (item 5) may be associated with their being strict disciplinarians and very concerned about spoiling babies.

No differences were found in the kinds and amount of baby equipment that should be used with babies. Similarly, no differences were reported in the numbers of toys that should be provided for children and in the way they should be combined with playmates.

All sixteen items in this file were summed and analyzed by a t-test. The result was a significant difference between the Black and white respondents (positive direction for the Blacks) at the .0002 level.

Religious Orientation

The sixteen questions in the file were planned to validate the hypothesis that a strong religious orientation is associated with Black families and child-rearing. Individuals tend to become more religious as they advance in age; therefore, finding a difference in the strength of this orientation among Black and white grandmothers would be particularly notable.

The following is a list of the questions in which a difference (positive for Blacks) was found, with the significance level noted:

(1) Of what religion are you a member? Black Afro-centric (p<.001). (A rating system developed by Dodson (1975) was utilized to code religion—for example, Baptist, A.M.E., Afro-centric, Lutheran, Episcopalian, Anglo-centric.)

(7) How long did your church service last?
   a. two hours   c. four-to-six hours
   b. three hours   d. all day
                          e. all day and evening
   Blacks longer—(p<.001)

(8) How long did you usually stay at church on Sunday (when your children were growing up)?
   a. two hours   d. all day
   b. three hours   e. all day and evening
   c. four-six hours
   Blacks longer—(p<.0001)

(9) Were you close to any families/individuals at your church?
   a. no   d. many
   b. one   e. fellowship like an
   c. a few   extended family
   Blacks reported a trend toward greater closeness to church members—not significant (p<.09).

(14) Did you know of any magical spiritual practices that can be helpful in times of trouble (seeing your psychic, working with roots, incantations)?

This item was designed to determine the extent to which the grandmothers were aware of folklore rather than to determine whether they personally believe in magic. Prompters were used of African-derived folklore reported by Herskovits (1958). They were coded a "yes" if they recognized the prompt or could elaborate upon it in a way similar to the responses of the South Carolina women. Blacks—yes (p<.0008).

The whites reported a positive tendency in one item:

(6) Did your church have special services for children?
   a. no
   b. yes
   whites—yes (p<.03)

All sixteen items in this file were summed and analyzed with a t-test. The result was an overall significant difference between the Black and the white respondents (a positive direction for the Blacks) at the .0001 level.

Autonomy/Discipline

A checklist was utilized in this dimension to determine whether a difference existed in the autonomy/freedom given to children by the grandmothers. They were asked to indicate an age at which children could play outside alone, go to parties, visit friends, and so forth. No differences were found between the judgments of the Black and the white grandmothers in the privileges accorded to boys or girls or in the ages at which the children were given freedom to participate in certain activities.

The subjects were asked to respond to a checklist of offenses that could elicit discipline. They were asked to indicate whether they would punish a child for an offense, and which of the following strategies they would use:

Corporal punishment (spanking)
Withdrawal of privileges (punishment)
Verbal disapproval (scolding)
Alternative strategy

The choices were coded on a scale from 0 to 4. If the subject did not punish a behavior, the response was coded zero; alternative strategy was coded 1; verbal disapproval was coded 2; withdrawal of privileges was coded 3; and corporal punishment was coded 4. Where two choices existed, the more severe was coded. The scores for the subjects were summed for each behavior, and a t-test was performed to determine whether the discipline of the grandmothers was more or less severe.

A significant difference was found in four of the thirteen behaviors. An additional one was marginally significant. The tendency for all dimensions was for the punishment of the Black grandmothers to be more severe. Listed below are the behaviors, with asterisks indicating those that were significant:

(1) soiling clothes
(2) destroying property
(3) stealing
(4) irresponsibility with money*
(5) disobeying*
(6) fighting
(7) eating wrong foods
(8) not eating meals
(9) lying
(10) irresponsibility with younger children
(11) not fighting back when assaulted*
(12) being disrespectful to elders*
(13) talking back to adults/parents*

The Black grandmothers placed the most emphasis upon disobedience, disrespect to elders, and talking back to adults. This was a consistent trend because those items cluster around respect and obedience. The property items were the first four, the one punished most severely was that dealing directly with money. This finding shows that in Black culture children must be trustworthy and able to handle money efficiently.

Item 11 (not fighting back when assaulted) elicited an interesting reaction from the white grandmothers. Many of them elaborated upon their choice by stating that they would punish a child *for* fighting back when assaulted. They felt that if their child were assaulted, the mother should contact the other child's parents. The Black grandmothers were very emphatic that a child should be able to defend himself and that the grandmothers would punish any child reluctant to do so.

The Black and white grandmothers reported equally on spanking their children. However, the Black grandmothers showed a significant choice of the switch, which has been identified by Herskovits (1958) as an African-derived instrument. He also found in his research that people of Africa and of the African diaspora tend to "whip" their children more than Europeans. The question was phrased: "Did you ever spank your child?" Perhaps a different phrasing of the question would have yielded more differences in the extent to which corporal punishment was applied. Inspecting the discipline chart discussed above shows that on at least five of the items that revealed differences, the Black grandmothers tended to apply corporal punishment for those offenses.

The respondents were asked whether they used different punishment instruments for different offenses, for example, spanking with the hand for a minor transgression and whipping with a belt for a major one. The white grandmothers showed a tendency to use different instruments that was marginally significant ($p < .09$). The Black grandmothers, on the other hand, showed a consistent preference for the switch.

Even though only four items on the discipline chart showed strong differences, and one showed marginally significant, the sum of the discipline chart revealed a significant overall difference ($p < .04$). This finding clearly indicates that the discipline styles of the two groups of women differ. This dimension should be investigated further because it has far-reaching implications for the manner in which Black children can be most effectively dealt with in school.

Willfulness/Assertiveness/Style

A popular hypothesis is that Black parents value idiosyncratic behavior from their children. I have developed this concept in the previous chapters. Young (1970) reports that Black infants are played with by their mothers in such a way that they are encouraged to be assertive; therefore, motives of willfulness are attributed to the actions of infants. Kochman (1969) suggested that "style" is very important in the Black community. "It is not only *what* you do, but *how* you do it that is important." The questions in this file, an initial attempt to analyze this complex dimension, were divided into four categories: idiosyncratic conception of children; aggression/confrontation; independence; and obedience. Although a sparse number of individual items revealed significant differences, the t-test of the sum of the overall file was significant (p < .02). The Blacks showed a tendency in the predicted direction. This dimension should be further investigated because it is salient to understanding how Black children behave.

One item in the group assessing the extent to which the grandmothers considered their children distinctive showed a trend the reverse of the prediction:

Do you feel now that your children resembled each other, or did they differ a great deal?
a. resembled each other more than they differed.
b. differed more than they resembled each other.

The white grandmothers reported significantly (p < .003) that their children differed more than they resembled each other.

In the items that were grouped as aggression/confrontation, the Black grandmothers reported a tendency in that direction in their own attitudes and in their children's behavior (in three out of six items). The items were as follows:

(10) Do you think that children need to know how to fight?
    a. no
    b. yes (but to defend themselves only)
    c. yes
    Blacks—yes (p < .07)
(11) What would you do if another child beat your child in a fight?
    a. reprimand child for fighting
    b. have father (someone) teach the child how to fight
    c. tell child not to let anyone defeat him again
    Blacks—positive toward child being able to fight (p < .0002)
(14) How did your children get along with their playmates?
    a. very well

b. occasional quarrels (and/or fights)
c. frequent quarrels (and/or fights)
Blacks—frequent quarrels (t-test p< .06; X^2 p< .05)

These items assert that Afro-Americans are an emotion-charged people. The Black grandmothers reported considerable tension among their children and their playmates but *not among siblings.*

As reported above in the discipline chart, Black grandmothers feel that children need to know how to fight; they would punish a child for not defending himself; and if their child were beaten by another child, they would tell the child not to let anyone defeat him again.

Two items classified under independence/obedience revealed differences in the Black and the white grandmothers' conceptions of permissiveness of verbal expression or tolerance for "talking back." One item approached significance and the other was significant.

(16) Some people think children who respect their parents would not talk back to them. Do you agree?
   a. yes, completely
   b. not entirely
   c. no (there are circumstances under which it is
      healthy for children to express themselves)
   Black responded yes, completely (p< .06)
(21) Do you think it is sassy for children to argue with their parents about rules?
   a. yes
   b. no
   Black—yes (p< .01)

These items reveal a low tolerance for "talking back" and arguing about rules. These data support the findings of Bonnie Thornton Dill (1980), who interviewed domestic Black women workers in white households. The Black women reported observing more permissiveness in the disciplinary styles of the white mothers. The white mothers envied the way the Black mothers commanded respect from their own children and the way in which they could command obedience in the white children, exceeding that of their own mothers.

Another item revealed a significant difference:

Did you ever require a younger child to obey an older sibling in the same way that she obeys a parent?
a. no
b. on certain occasions
c. yes, most of the time

Blacks—yes, most of the time (p<.01)

This item refers to the organization in Black families (particularly large Black families) that requires older siblings to take frequent responsibility for younger children. Therefore, a "pecking order" exists that may have African roots but certainly grows out of the intricacies of the Afro-American life. Black parents must socialize their children to obey older siblings as they would a parent so that they can be cared for and disciplined effectively when the parents are not present.

Creative Arts

Researchers have claimed that children in the Black community are involved in the creative arts to a greater degree than white children. I have suggested in earlier chapters (through analysis of the work of Rosalie Cohen and others) that Black people tend to be very expressive and creative in the arts. The questions in this file, designed to explicate that involvement, were grouped into three categories:

(1) Music/Dance/TV
(2) Fashion Arts
(3) Visual Arts

The t-test was performed for the sum of each category and for the overall file of creative arts. The findings are summarized below:

(1) Music/Dance/TV
    Blacks in the predicted direction (p<.002)
(2) Fashion Arts not significant (p<.18)
(3) Visual Arts
    Blacks in the predicted direction (p<.04)
(4) Total of the sums (Creative Arts)
    Blacks in the predicted direction (p<.0009)

Music/Dance/TV

Two questions were asked to identify differences in musical preferences among the Black and white respondents. A chi-square distribution was obtained on the choices. The findings from both items were significant. The data are summarized in Tables 13 and 14.

The white grandmothers show a definite tendency to state music preferences that are Anglo-centric (choices one through four). Even though the choices of the Black grandmothers are distributed over the Anglo and Afro types of music, they still show a significant ten-

Table 13

Favorite Type of Music

Type of Music	White		Black	
	No.	%	No.	%
Classical	4	26.67	2	13.33
Country & Western	3	20		
Religious (mainstream)	1	6		
American popular (Frank Sinatra)	7	46.67	2	13.33
Rock				
Disco			2	13.33
Rhythm and Blues			3	20.00
Gospel			5	33.33
Jazz				

t-test of item $p < .0003$.
Chi-square distribution $p < .01$.

Table 14

Type of Music of Favorite
Recording Artist

Types of Music	White		Black	
	No.	%	No.	%
Classical	2	13.33	1	6.67
Country and Western	2	13.33		
Religious			3	6.67
American popular	11	73.33	1	6.67
Rock				
Disco				
Rhythm and Blues			6	40.00
Gospel			5	33.33
Jazz			1	6.67

t-test of item $p < .0001$.
Chi-square distribution $p < .006$.

dency to cluster around the Afro-centric music (choices seven through nine). This finding is an example of the extent to which Black people are more bicultural than whites. The contrast between the white and Black respondents is even more focused (summarized in Table 14) in the question concerning naming a favorite recording artist.

Six questions were asked about enjoyment of dancing. One item that reversed the prediction for whites approaches significance:

(4) Do you like to dance?

    a. no

b. yes, when I was young
c. yes, now
whites—positive ($0 < .09$)

In two items of the six, Blacks were favorable toward dancing:

(8) Did your children dance when they were growing up?
a. no
b. yes
Blacks—positive ($p < .03$)
(9) Did they enjoy dancing?
a. no
b. yes
Blacks—positive ($p < .01$)

Three items did not reveal a significant difference among the respondents but did predict race in a step-wise regression equation.

(7) Did your children see you dance when they were growing up?
a. no
b. yes
(Blacks positive)
(10) Did they listen to music?
a. no
b. sometimes
c. often
(Blacks slightly more positive)

No significant differences were found in the items related to television viewing.

Fashion Arts
Nine questions were asked to determine whether differences existed between Blacks and whites in adorning the body. It had been hypothesized that Black children are very stylistic and particular in their selection of clothing and in their preferences for colors. This hypothesis was not supported by the responses to the questions of this study.

Visual Arts
The questions in this category were designed to identify differences in the display of pictures and symbols in the household. No difference was found in the total number of pictures displayed in an artistic fashion (including calendars). There was also no difference in the number of religious pictures or symbols displayed.

However, a significant difference was found in the number of racial/political pictures displayed. The significance level was $p < .03$

in a positive trend for the Black respondents. The Black grand mothers were more prone to display pictures of Black heroes, such as Martin Luther King, Jr. and white political leaders who were popular with Black people, such as John F. Kennedy and Robert F. Kennedy. The white grandmothers did not report a tendency to display patriotic symbols, such as the American flag or political pictures, such as a picture of the President of the United States.

Drawing upon the literature (Nobles 1974b) that suggests strong family ties are rooted in an African heritage, I hypothesized that this orientation would be expressed in the display of pictures of family members and friends.

Blacks showed a tendency to display pictures of family members that approached significance ($p < .07$). Blacks also showed a significant tendency to display the pictures of friends ($p < .05$).

Food Preference

This file consisted of a checklist designed to determine whether there are differences between the food preferences of the Black and the white respondents. The point has been made elsewhere (Hale 1981) that cultural preferences in foods should be considered in planning nutrition programs for children in early childhood educational settings.

The checklist was adapted from the work of Jualynne Dodson (1975) who sought to classify foods, spices, and methods of preparation into Afro- and Anglo-centric categories. The foods listed include a number of items that are popular in the Black community. The white grandmothers were asked to list additional foods. They did add many, which were not analyzed in this study because all the subjects did not have an equal opportunity to consider them. These items will be included in a revised version of the instrument for a future study. Listed below are the findings of seven categories that were analyzed:

(1) Meats

The sum of the meats approached significance ($p < .09$) in a positive direction for Blacks. Blacks showed a preference for the following meats:

    chitterlings ($p < .01$)
    neck bones ($p < .01$)
    lamb ($p < .004$)

(2) Salads

The sum of the salads was not significant ($p < .63$). No individual salad was significant.

(3) Spices

The sum of the spices was significant (p<.007) in a positive direction for the Blacks. Blacks showed a preference for the following spices:

black pepper (p<.06)
sage (p<.01)
thyme (p<.07)
Accent (p<.02)

(4) Vegetables

The sum of the vegetables was not significant (p<.30). However, Blacks showed a significant preference for certain vegetables:

okra (p<.04)
collard greens (p<.0001)
broccoli (p<.01)
spinach (p<.01)
cabbage (p<.04)

(5) Breads

The sum of breads was not significant (p<.46). However, two of the breads were significantly preferred by Blacks:

corn bread (p<.004)
rolls (p<.01)

(6) Starches

The sum of starches was significant (p<.05) in a positive direction for Blacks. Only one item individually approaches significance. Potato (p<.07) was preferred by Blacks.

(7) Sandwiches

The sum of sandwiches was not significant (p<.73). Two types of sandwiches—tuna salad and bologna—were included in the stepwise regression equation as predictors of race. They were both slightly preferred by whites.

Cooking Methods of Chicken and Beef Steak

From nine choices, the respondents were asked to indicate the methods of cooking they frequently used with chicken and beefsteak.

The t-test of the sum of the chicken choices was significant, showing a higher mean for Black respondents (p<.03). One method (frying) was significantly preferred by Blacks (p<.03). Another method (stewing) approached significance (p<.06) and was preferred by Blacks.

Two methods (boiling and simmering) were not found by the t-test to be significant. They were slightly preferred by whites.

The t-test performed on the sum of the beefsteak choices found the differences to be nonsignificant (p<.90). One method (sautéing) approached significance (p<.07) and was preferred by the white respondents.

Attitudes Toward Abortion/Conception
The questions in this file were designed to determine whether a difference existed in the attitudes of the respondents toward abortion and toward ways of handling conception for a child out of wedlock.

A significant difference was found in the sum of the four questions in the file (p<.02). I predicted that Black women would be less in favor of abortion and more tolerant toward keeping babies born out of wedlock. This tendency was supported.

The t-test and the chi-square distribution reported significant differences on two items. The results are summarized in Tables 15 and 16.

Part 2

Physical Activity
I have suggested that Black children are physically precocious at birth and through the age of three. The questions in this file were designed to identify any differences in the ways in which Black and white babies are handled that may account for this precocity. The questions were organized into three categories: feeding, toileting, and movement. The t-test on the sum of the entire file was nonsignificant (p<.66). The mean was higher for the white respondents—the reverse of the prediction.

Table 15

Response to Question Three
(Abortion/Conception)

3. What would you recommend to your daughter if she conceived a child out of wedlock?

	White		Black	
	No.	%	No.	%
no response	2	15.38		
recommend an abortion	2	15.38		
pressure her to get married	2	15.38		
have baby and give it up for adoption	2	15.38	1	6.67
raise the baby yourself	3	23.08	4	26.67
have daughter raise the baby	1	7.69	8	53.33
mother and daughter raise the baby	3	23.08	2	13.33

X^2(p<.07); t-test (p<.03)

Table 16

Responses to Question Four
(Abortion/Conception)

4. What would you recommend to your son if he conceived a child out of wedlock?

	White		Black	
	No.	%	No.	%
no response	2	15.38	1	6.67
recommend an abortion	2	15.38		
pressure him to get married	4	30.77	1	6.67
girlfriend give baby up for adoption	3	23.08		
raise the baby yourself			3	20.00
girlfriend raise baby, son support child	3	23.08	10	66.67
girlfriend and her mother raise baby	1	7.69		

$X^2 (p<.01)$; t-test $(p<.01)$

We found no significant items in the feeding category; however, we found one significant item in the toileting category:

(4) Should you spank a baby if he makes a mistake? (during toilet training)
Blacks—yes $(p<.03)$

This response correlates with attitudes reported above of an orientation toward strict discipline and corporal punishment.

Some interesting findings surfaced in the movement category. The t-test revealed a younger age of walking for Black babies $(p<.005)$. The mean for Blacks was ten months and the mean for whites was twelve months. The chi-square distribution showed a significant difference in the age of creeping; Blacks creep at a younger age $(p<.04)$.

The white mothers seemed to be less "gadget" oriented in assisting their children to walk. The responses to the item that follows approached significance on a t-test:

(2) Should mothers do things to help their babies walk?
   a. yes, buy special shoes, walkers
   b. yes, give them practice
   c. no, just give them the freedom to move
      and they will walk when they are ready.
   Whites—freedom to move $(p<.06)$

The Black respondents were slightly more oriented toward permitting the child to crawl on the floor (most of them added, "If it were clean").

(3) Should babies be permitted to crawl on the floor?
   a. no
   b. yes, sometimes
   c. yes, as much as they wish
   Blacks—positive (p< .08)

The subjects were asked whether they would use playpens, walkers, strollers, and carriages with their children. The only significant difference was that the Blacks expressed a preference for baby carriages (p<.01).

Social Breadth

Researchers had hypothesized that the Black family has a larger network of family and friends they rely upon and interact with. The questions in this file were designed to explicate these relationships. The t-test of the sum of the questions in this file was nonsignificant even though the mean for the Blacks was slightly higher (p<.88).

Five items approached significance, and one was significant, but fewer of them reversed the prediction:

(5) Do you have any friends you either regarded as family or gave kinship titles to (cousin, aunt, sister, mother)?
   a. no   d. 3
   b. 1   e. 4 or more
   c. 2
   Whites—higher (p<.09) t-test

(7) Do you have any friends you traded child care with?
   a. no   d. 3
   b. 1   e. 4 or more
   c. 2
   Whites—higher (p<.06) X^2

(8) Which did you prefer to care for your children: a friend or a relative?
   a. relative
   b. friend
   Whites—friend (p<.08) X^2

(15) How many friends did you correspond with?
   a. 1   d 3
   b. 2   e. 4 or more
   c. 2
   Blacks—higher (p<.06) t-test

(19) How many of your neighbors did you know pretty well?
    a. none   d. 3 + (several)
    b. 1   e. all
    c. 2
    Blacks—higher ($p < .07$) t-test

(20) Did you exchange favors with them?
    a. no   c. often
    b. occasionally
    Whites—higher ($p < .04$) t-test

Achievement Orientation

Researchers hypothesized that Blacks have a high achievement orientation. The t-test of the sum of the file did not support the prediction ($p < .22$). The mean for the Blacks was slightly higher.

Of the twenty-two items in this file two were significant and four approached significance (all in the predicted direction).

(3) When your children were growing up, did you have any ideas about the kind of future work you wanted them to do?
    a. no
    b. yes (above a certain status level)
    c. yes (definite occupations)
    Blacks showed a tendency toward specific preferences for their children ($p < .09$).

(4) Did you have any ideas about the kind of work you did not want your child to do?
    a. no
    b. yes (certain low status work)
    c. yes (certain occupation)
    Blacks showed a tendency to shun hard, menial jobs or to mention occupations such as domestic work ($p < .06$).

(5) Did you expect your daughters to be employed after marriage?
    a. no
    b. yes
    Blacks—yes ($p < .02$)

(7) Did you work regularly when your children were growing up?
    a. no
    b. yes
    Whites worked less ($p < .004$).

(10) Do you feel that you have been able to accomplish the aspirations or plans with which both of you started your family?
    a. no
    b. yes
    Blacks—no ($p < .06$)

136

(12) How important do you feel education has been in the life of your children? The responses are summarized in Table 17.

Table 17

Responses to Question Twelve
(Achievement Orientation)

12. How important do you feel that education has been in the life of your children?

	Whites		Blacks	
	No.	%	No.	%
not particularly important	1	6.67	1	6.67
somewhat important	7	46.67	1	6.67
very important	7	46.67	13	86.67

Chi-square (p<.04) (Blacks higher)

No significant difference appeared in the report of the respondents about aspirations for male and female children; age of marriage and childbearing; desires of their children about attending college; plans they made to finance their children's college education; their own enjoyment of reading; and the frequency with which they read to their children.

The responses to item 1 (below) were nonsignificant. However, both the Black and the white grandmothers aspire for a similar level of education for their children.

(1) What was the minimum level of education you wanted your children to receive? The responses are summarized in Table 18.

Variability of Home Environment

Researchers hypothesized that the number of people in the Black household and the ways in which routines were performed would create a high degree of variability. This hypothesis was not supported overall by the questions in the file. The t-test of the sum (26 questions) was nonsignificant (p<.86), although the mean for the Blacks was higher. Three items were found to be significant, according to the t-test. The Blacks' meals, eaten together, were more prone to vary.

The Black respondents were more prone to have reared children who were not their own and to be engaged presently in child care:

(25) Did you rear any children other than your own?
   a. no
   b. yes
   Blacks—yes (p<.04) t-test

Table 18

Responses to Question One
(Achievement Orientation)

1. What was the minimum level of education that you wanted your children to receive?

	Whites		Blacks	
	No.	%	No.	%
no minimum (whatever they wanted)	1	6.67	1	6.67
read and write				
grade school			1	6.67
high school	4	26.67	5	33.33
college	10	66.67	8	53.33
graduate school				

Chi-square (p<.72)

(26) Do you now care for any children? (babysit, foster mother)
  a. no
  b. yes
  Blacks—yes (p<.0009) t-test

A chi-square analysis showed more variability among Blacks on two items:

(12) Did your school-age children do the same things after school each day, or did their activities change from day to day?
  a. same things every day
  b. same things most days
  c. same things on week days, different on weekends (whites)
  d. different things on most days (Blacks)
  e. different things every day
  Blacks showed a tendency toward more variability (p<.04)

(17) How would you describe the number of visitors your household received daily (including children)?
  a. no visitors
  b. few visitors (1–3) (whites)
  c. several visitors (3–7)
  d. many visitors (7–15) (Blacks)
  e. constant visitors (15+)
  The whites clustered around few visitors and the Blacks clustered around several and many visitors (p<.01).

(22) How many children did you adopt or provide foster care for?

a. one

b. two

c. three

d. four

e. five or more

The mean for both groups was two (nonsignificant difference).

Variability of Home Environment Chart

The subjects were given a list of activities children could engage in after school each day. They were asked to enter the number of days a week their children participated in those activities. The t-test was performed for the sum of the chart, and there was not an overall significant difference ($p<.20$). Analysis of the individual items reveals the following:

(1) The white children were more prone to listen to the radio ($p<.04$) and engage in free play ($p<.002$).

(2) The Black children were more prone to visit friends ($p<.01$), sleep ($p<.002$), and perform household chores ($p<.001$).

(3) Homework was included with the above-mentioned significant items in the step-wise regression equation. It was nonsignificant ($p<.40$), but a slight tendency showed for the Blacks to do homework more than the whites.

(4) The items for which there were no significant differences were club meetings, music lessons, dance, hobbies, work for money, reading, and sports.

Adaptability of Family Roles

Researchers hypothesized that Black families have a fluid system of performing child-care tasks and household chores. Three questions were asked to determine whether household chores were divided into distinctive roles for men and women. A nonsignificant difference showed in the t-test concerning the sum of these questions ($p<.23$). The three questions revealed nonsignificant differences, with only one approaching significance.

(1) Do you feel that males and females should perform distinctive household tasks?

a. yes

b. no

The whites tended to respond no to a greater extent, but the difference was nonsignificant ($p<.42$).

(2) Did you ever have your son do something that his father did not have to do (wash dishes, for example)?

A very slight tendency existed for the Blacks to respond yes. The difference was miniscule and nonsignificant ($p<.86$).

(3) Did you ever have your daughter do something that you did not
do (cut grass, for example)?
a. no
b. yes
The whites showed a tendency to respond yes that approached
significance (p<.06).

Child-Care Tasks and Household-Tasks Charts
The respondents were asked to indicate on a checklist what person or combination of persons performed tasks associated with
child care and housekeeping. The t-test for the sum of the child-
care tasks was nonsignificant (p<.13). The t-test for the sum of the
housekeeping tasks was also nonsignificant (p<.56).

The purpose of the checklist was to determine whether the
mother was performing most of the tasks or whether other family
members participated. The choices were coded in such a way that a
low mean indicated a low participation by other family members.

On the child-care tasks checklist four items (out of nineteen) revealed significant differences, according to the t-test, and one item
that approached significance. These items all showed adaptability
in the performance of child-care tasks in the white family. No item
showed greater participation in the Black family. The items are as
follows:

1. preparing child's breakfast (p<.06)
7. putting child to bed (p<.02)
11. driving child to school and/or other activities (p<.002)
16. shopping for playthings (p<.0002)
17. shopping for school supplies (p<.005)

On the housekeeping-tasks checklist two items (out of twenty-
seven) showed significant differences, according to the t-test. These
two items showed greater participation in the Black families. None
showed greater participation in the white families:

(1) cleaning oven and refrigerator
(13) ironing

A chi-square distribution was also obtained for each item on the
checklist to determine whether a difference existed in the distribution of the tasks.

On the child-care-tasks checklist, only one item was added to
those that the t-test found significant.

(13) taking the child to doctor/dentist appointments (p<.02)

The Black grandmothers (93 percent) took the child themselves, and 53 percent of the white grandmothers took their children. Twenty percent were carried by the white fathers and mothers.

On the housekeeping-tasks checklist two items were significant, and two approached significance in addition to "ironing" that the t-test found significant.

(2) washing dishes (p <.03)
(9) washing floors (p< .07)
(11) cleaning bathroom (p< .07)
(27) figuring income tax (p< .08)

When the tasks were shared, a tendency existed for them to be shared by the husband in the white family and by the children or other relatives in the Black family. In the item on income-tax preparation, the majority of the white grandmothers reported that either their husbands did it or they hired help. The Black grandmothers reported that they either did it themselves or hired help. A clear tendency in the data seemed to be greater involvement by white husbands in the work of the household.

That the sums of each checklist were nonsignificant indicates the validity of the impression of the investigator as the data were collected that the women in both groups were responsible for the bulk of the work.

Discussion

This study should be conceptualized as a first step toward elucidating values that reflect an Afro-centric orientation expressed in the socialization of children. Child-rearing takes place within the family and thus is a key indicator of cultural values. Generating the twelve files of this study is an attempt to analyze the ethos of the Afro-American community, which converges on the children to produce distinctive behavioral and expressive styles.

This line of research is difficult because it is groundbreaking. No coherent base of social science research serves as the hypothetical framework. The research that exists has been supplemented by literary, folkloric sources. The attempt to extract psychological meaning from the creative arts is in its infancy, and the data are fragmented at best.

Even with the tenuousness of the hypotheses of this study, seven of the overall twelve files reflected significant differences in the responses of the Black and the white grandmothers. In many of the significant files, few of the individual items were significant. However, enough variance existed that it was reflected in the sum of the file. This variance may be accounted for by the small number of subjects; or it may be that the concept represented by the file is salient, but we need to devise more sensitive questions in order to analyze the concept precisely.

In the five files that did not reveal significant differences, individual items were significant, a fact that suggested the need to narrow either the concept or the orientation.

In the section below we will discuss the results of this study and make suggestions for further research.

Human Orientation vs. Object Orientation; Social Breadth; Variability of Home Environment; Attitudes toward Abortion and Conception.
These four files are discussed together because they are designed to conceptualize the realms of feeling that arise from interpersonal relations thought to have important implications for Black people.

The questions about massaging the baby to shape its appearance reveal a distinctive difference in the way Black mothers believe babies should be handled. It seems possible, as we have mentioned, that this practice is an example of an African retention, a concept that should be explained further because it may provide a clue to the physical precocity of Black infants. In other words, the explanation may not lie exclusively in genetic explanations but also in the ways Black women handle their babies.

This "human orientation" was not expressed by the Black grandmothers in a tendency to be responsive to a crying baby or to hold a baby a great deal. The white grandmothers did, however, show a tendency in that direction. The concept seems to be related to the Black grandmothers' ideas about discipline. They were concerned about "spoiling" babies and felt that being too responsive or holding the babies too often would interfere with the kind of discipline they wished to impose.

A surprising finding was that no difference existed in the extent to which the Black and the white grandmothers valued objects and gadgets associated with child-rearing (toys and baby equipment). Observations of Black and of white households suggest differences in the number of toys provided to Black and white children (Young 1970). Perhaps a gap exists between what is valued and what is practiced that can be filled only by combining interview with observation.

Attitudes revealed in the abortion/conception file are related to "human orientation." First of all, we attempted to secure Protestant subjects in order to control differences that might be caused by religious orientation. New Haven has a very large Catholic population; it became difficult to secure the desired ethnic stratification and religious singularity among white subjects. Therefore, a number of

Catholics were included in the study and had some influence on the responses in this file. I noticed a tendency for the Black subjects to be against abortion, but they would tolerate it for the first three reasons mentioned: life of the mother in danger; rape or incest; deformed baby. The white Protestant women showed a tendency to allow abortion and to include the other three reasons as valid: mother not married; unable to support baby financially; mother doesn't want to have a baby. The investigator noticed that this began to change as the number of white Catholic subjects increased. They tended to object to abortion and not to agree that any circumstances for having one were valid. This tendency seems to account for the nonsignificant difference for those two questions. Another interesting observation was that many of the grandmothers were not aware that deformity of a fetus could be detected before birth.

The responses to the question about handling a child conceived out of wedlock support the findings of other research on this issue (Hill 1972). The Black grandmothers differed from the white in not recommending abortion, pressured marriage, or adoption. They seemed most oriented toward the girl's keeping the baby and rearing it, with support from her mother and the baby's father. This is a pervasive attitude among Afro-Americans. Even though premarital conception is discouraged, any baby is accepted.

The social breadth and variability of home environment files are related to each other and to human orientation in some aspects. Social breadth had to do with the extent to which the nuclear family is a part of a broader network of extended family members and friends who provide support and assistance. One dimension of the variability of the home environment was related to the numbers of people who lived in the household and to the number who visited.

The findings of these two files were nonsignificant overall, but some items supported the hypothesis. Under social breadth, the Blacks tended to correspond with more friends and to know more of their neighbors than the whites. The whites tended, however, to exchange favors more often with their neighbors. Contrary to the prediction, the white grandmothers showed more social breadth on four out of six items that revealed significant differences.

In the variability of the home environment file, the Black grandmothers reported that they reared children other than their natural children significantly more than did the white grandmothers. They also tended to provide present care for children through babysitting or foster mothering. This item was included in the variability file because it added to the human change in the environment and the stimulation the children received from interacting intimately with other children. However, this willingness to rear other people's children is not unrelated to social breadth, attitude toward abortion/conception, and human orientation. Robert Hill (1973) has suggested that a strength of Black families is the willingness of Black people to "informally adopt" children. He concludes that it was once thought Black people did not adopt children. However, the fact is they don't patronize *adoption agencies*. Many of the women who rear foster children are middle-aged; some are single and lower-income. They would be rejected by an adoption agency as an adoptive parent. However, these women will often rear a child of a daughter who bore the baby out of wedlock or will take in the child of a friend or a neighbor who needs assistance. Hill suggests that providing foster care or adoptive parenting would be improved if these cultural styles were implemented.

In the file on variability of home environment, Blacks reported having significantly more daily visitors. They reported also that their school-age children engaged in different activities on most days, whereas the whites said their children did similar things on weekdays. Some difference was reported in the kinds of activities the Black and white children participated in after school. White children were more prone to listen to the radio and to engage in free play. Black children were more prone to visit friends and to perform household chores. No differences showed in their tendency to participate in the following: club meetings, music lessons, dance, hobbies, work for money, reading, and sports.

Significant variability was reported in the mealtime behavior in the Black family, as was greater fluidity concerning who ate together at certain meals.

Although the overall variability file was not significant, some interesting items warranted further investigation of this concept. A more precise study should be made of how the Black home environment is organized and what kinds of activities Black children engage in. Enough evidence in this study could guide future efforts.

Autonomy/Discipline; Willfulness/Assertiveness/Style

An analysis of these two files shows a definite tendency toward distinct cultural values related to discipline in child-rearing. The Black grandmothers were more prone to use corporal punishment than the whites. More specifically, they reported using the switch, an Afro-centric instrument of punishment. The white grandmothers reported varying the instrument with the offense when corporal punishment was used.

In both the discipline and willfulness files, the Black grandmothers reported severe compliance demands around obedience offenses. They felt strongly that children should be punished for talking back to adults, for disrespect of elders, for disobeying adults, for disobeying older siblings, for being irresponsible with money, and for not fighting back when assaulted. They punished irresponsibility with money more than they did other property offenses, such as soiling clothes. They also felt strongly that Black children need to know how to fight (mostly to defend themselves). The white grandmothers disapproved of fighting and felt that if a child were molested, the grandmothers would talk to the offending child's parents. This difference in child-rearing values has been discussed earlier.

An interesting finding was that the Black grandmothers reported their children had frequent quarrels with playmates but not with their siblings. Clearly the prediction that a confrontation/aggression orientation exists among Black children was supported.

No clear differences were found in the amount of autonomy/independence afforded to Black children.

The attempt to determine the existence of an idiosyncratic conception of children was problematic. Contrary to the prediction, the white grandmothers reported their children to be distinct and unique. This concept was related to "style," which is thought to characterize Black behavior. This whole concept of willfulness/assertiveness/style was supported in overall difference, but it should be investigated further so that its elements can be explained with more precision.

Religious Orientation

"A strong religious orientation," cited by Robert Hill (1972) as a strength of Black families, is important on two levels. The first is that the church serves as a kind of extended family providing material, human, and ideological support in the socialization of children. This function is discussed in more detail elsewhere (Hale 1977a). Second, religious conceptualizations form a unifying thread through the culture of a people because it gives their ethos form and substance.

The questions in the religious orientation file only scratch the surface of identifying differences in Afro-American and Euro-American conceptions of the universe. John Mbiti (1970) has done groundbreaking work in systematizing African religions and philosophies. Wade Nobles, Na'im Akbar, and others have begun the process of articulating a Black psychology that emerges from a distinctly Afro-centric world view. This is a fertile area for further research.

This file showed a significant difference (when summed) between the Black and white respondents. The Blacks were members of

Afro-centric religious organizations (Baptist, African Methodist Episcopal) and the whites were members of Anglo/Euro-centric religions (Episcopalian, Presbyterian, and so forth).

The church services of the Black subjects lasted longer, and Blacks spent more time at church on Sundays. They also showed a tendency toward greater closeness to the members of their churches. The white subjects reported that their churches had special services for children.

The Black grandmothers were familiar with folklore that originated in Africa. Through the work of Melville Herskovits (1958) and interviews with Black women in South Carolina, I was able to prompt the subjects to determine whether they had heard of various stories and whether they could elaborate upon them. I noted a striking difference between the two groups in terms of familiarity with these "magical/spiritual" practices. For example, a story tells about babies being born with a "veil" on their faces. This veil is actually a thin membrane. Such a child is said to be able to "see spirits" or to see the future. The mother keeps the membrane, and various stories tell about how she can detect the health and well-being of the child by examining the texture and complexion of the "veil." An elaboration on the story originally obtained in South Carolina was that some children became frightened by their ability to see the spirits; so the mother could prepare a tea to "blind" the child (that is, to end his ability to see the spirits). The mother had to prepare this tea and dip the membrane in it and have the child drink it.

The majority of the Black grandmothers disclaimed believing in these stories or practicing magic, and many were reticent to admit having heard of the stories. A great deal of restating and prompting was necessary. One informer from South Carolina suggested that the Black people in the Sea Islands area are very protective of their culture, and what appears to be a lack of familiarity is really an unwillingness to be revealing. That element may have been operating in New Haven with the Black grandmothers.

Several of the white grandmothers were able to share folklore from their ethnic heritage, and I recorded it to determine whether any common stories would emerge. I did not notice any commonalities. The lack of familiarity of the white grandmothers with the African stories was striking. This is further evidence that aspects of African culture have been retained by Afro-Americans.

Creative Arts

The responses in this file indicate Afro-centric and Euro-centric musical forms. The white grandmothers preferred classical, country and western, religious (represented by George Beverly Shea), and

American popular as their favorite. None chose rock and disco. None of the white grandmothers indicated choices that were distributed over the Afro- and Anglo-centric musical types. The Blacks clustered around the Afro-centric forms: disco (bi-cultural) rhythm and blues, gospel, and jazz. The majority selected rhythm and blues and gospel. Even though the Black respondents were more bicultural than the whites, they still made Afro-centric musical choices.

There was a tendency for the Blacks to enjoy dancing and listening to music even though some individual items were contrary to the trends. When questioned about teaching their children to dance, one grandmother smiled and said with a chuckle, "You don't have to teach colored children to dance!" The responses to these questions clearly indicate that music and dancing are pervasive in the Black home environment.

One interesting finding was no difference in the attitudes of the grandmothers toward television viewing of children. One explanation may be that their own children were reared before television, so they reported on their beliefs (which often are idealized) rather than their practices.

No significant differences appeared in the fashion arts file overall and no significance on the individual items. These findings were surprising because we had hypothesized that Afro-Americans (as a part of the African heritage) are very fashion conscious and are oriented toward adornment with clothing, creative hairstyles, jewelry, hats, and scarves. This dimension should be investigated in the future with questions that are more precise.

The visual arts category was a beginning effort to understand the Black home environment. The responses indicated that Blacks are more prone to displaying pictures of figures in Black history (such as Dr. Martin Luther King) and political figures popular among Blacks (such as President John F. Kennedy) than are whites. Blacks also have a tendency to display pictures of family members and friends. No difference was apparent in the number of pictures displayed artistically in the Black and the white families nor in the number of religious symbols displayed. Future research should investigate other aspects of the Black home environment, such as space utilization, colors of walls, floors and furnishings, types of playthings, and so forth. Such a study may deepen our understanding of the culture of the home and improve the continuity we can provide at school.

Food Preference

The food preference file was only marginally successful. The major contribution of this study was to improve the instrument. Most of the foods listed were those that were felt to be Afro-centric. The white grandmothers added items to the list. However, those foods were not included in the analysis because all subjects did not have an equal opportunity to respond. The instrument will be expanded for future research.

The only significant categories of foods were spices, starches, and cooking methods. Individual items within the other categories were also significant. The findings of this study suggest that the following foods and spices are Afro-centric: chitterlings, neckbones, lamb, black pepper, sage, thyme, Accent, okra, collard greens, broccoli, spinach, cabbage, cornbread, rolls, and potatoes. Blacks also prefer to fry and stew chicken. Whites prefer to sauté beefsteak.

Further investigation of cultural preferences in food is important in designing nutritional curricula for early-childhood education programs. A popular slogan says, "What you eat is what you are." If that is true, study of the nutritional environment of Black children may be important in interpreting their behavior. This study of Afro-American food preference should encompass food selection, preparation, and spicing. It should show definite trends in areas common to Black people and related to the African heritage. This information would have obvious implications for health services. However, it would also be helpful to those planning nutritional curricula for Black children in the schools. Many day-care and child-development programs design their menus from nutrition manuals with little understanding of the nutritional preferences of children that have been shaped by their culture. Many of the meals prepared in institutional settings are rejected by children. This may be an area in which school is defined by some children as a strange and alien environment.

Physical Activity

The questions in the physical activity file were designed to explain possible reasons for the physical precocity of Black infants. We were interested in how the mother handled physical functions and in the extent to which she used gadgets.

The overall file was not significant when it was summed. We found almost no differences between Blacks and whites in feeding practices and beliefs. The only toileting difference is that Black mothers are willing to spank a baby during toilet training. This finding is consistent with others that reflect a tendency for Blacks to use corporal punishment.

The Black grandmothers report an earlier age of creeping and walking for their children than did the white grandmothers. Contrary to the prediction, the white grandmothers were less likely to value gadgets such as special shoes or walkers to assist the child to learn to walk. They believed that, given the freedom to move, the infants would walk when they were ready. The Blacks were somewhat more prone to let their children crawl on the floor (when it was clean). In terms of gadgets related to movement, the only preference was that Blacks favor baby carriages.

The findings in this file were disappointing. I believe there are differences in physical activity that were not captured. One area that related to the massage, shaping, and handling of the baby was included in the human orientation file and may have weakened the physical activity file. More precision in analyzing this realm is clearly called for.

Achievement Orientation

Robert Hill (1972) has suggested that Black families have a strong achievement orientation. The findings of this study support his analysis, but this orientation is not significantly *stronger* than that of the whites. The Black respondents also had a clearer conception of the type of work they did *not* want their children to do (hard, menial jobs or domestic work) than of specific occupations they aspired to for their children.

The realities of Black life are reflected in the finding that the Black grandmothers expected their daughters to be employed after marriage—a finding significantly different from that of the white grandmothers. The Black women also significantly reported working while rearing their children—in contrast to the white women.

The Black grandmothers also expressed more dissatisfaction with their ability to accomplish the aspirations they and their husbands had when they started their family. They expressed the importance of education in the lives of their children, a statement significantly different from that of the white grandmothers.

A number of questions included in this file related to achievement, such as age of marriage, did not elicit significantly different responses from the two groups. These items contributed to the overall nonsignificance of the file. However, some of the items show that Black women value education and hard work because they know how easy it is for Black youths to be tracked into low status, low-paying, hard-labor jobs. They clearly place a strong emphasis on securing an education as an aid to upward mobility. The fact, however, that the women could more clearly articulate the kind of work they did *not* want their children to do is symptomatic of a dilemma most Black (particularly lower-income) children are confronted with. They are constantly urged to have high aspirations, but they do not have the opportunity to get to know models of success. They also do not receive enough support at critical times to be able to construct a step-by-step life plan that will lead to success. In other words, many Black parents verbally tell their children to be successful, but they do not know how to assist their children to implement the mechanisms of success.

Adaptability of Family Roles

Robert Hill (1972) has suggested that a strength of Black families is adaptability of family roles. That is, family members are more willing than whites to be flexible in the tasks they perform in order that functions of the family be fulfilled. Although no overall significant differences showed in the responses of the two groups in terms of the performance of child care and household tasks, the chi-square distribution showed that when responsibilities were shared, the white husbands participated more than the Black husbands. When tasks were shared in the Black household, they were most often performed by the children and sometimes by other relatives. However, usually the women in both groups performed most of the tasks associated with child care and housekeeping. The findings of this study did not support Hill's analysis.

Seven

Toward A Curriculum Relevant to Afro-Americans: Implications for Early Childhood Education

I ask you my children

What did you learn today
did anyone tell you how to meet tomorrow
did anyone tell you why there are people
who don't know you . . . .

did anyone seem to know who you were
did anyone know that you have the blood of Africa
in your veins
or did they pretend to be blind to your color and thereby
deny its value

What did you learn . . . .

did anyone explain the nature of freedom
did anyone explain the nature of racism . . . .

did anyone explain the nature of love
did anyone know anything about those things
did anyone know anything
What did you learn today?

—Ronald Coleman*

In this chapter the threads that have been woven through the previous chapters will be brought together. A great deal of work needs

---

*From a 1977 calendar, "Black Children Just Keep on Growing."

151

What did you learn today?

to be done to the foundation for an alternative educational process for Black children. However, I will describe an early-education model for preschoolers that emerges from the thesis of this book. Hypothetical plans are under way to pilot this model in Mississippi. It is written in such a way that early childhood teachers will be motivated to innovate, and potential scholars will receive suggestions to direct future research efforts in this area.

Educational Philosophy

Three components are ideal for a curriculum for Black children:

1. Political/cultural (ideology)
2. Pedagogical relevance (method)
3. Academic rigor (content)

Political/cultural ideology. An alternative curricular model for Afro-American children must have at its foundation an accurate historical and political analysis of the situation of Black people in America and in the world.

Tillman and Tillman (1969) have concluded that Black people, wherever they are found in the world, are in a colonial relationship

with white people (Europeans). This colonial system has perpetuated their political, economic, and cultural exploitation. Regardless
of the continent on which it is found—America, Africa, the Caribbean, the system achieves the same end: exploiting the labor power
and resources of the colonized.

The Tillmans suggest further that the form of this exploitation in
America was slavery, but when slavery ended, it was replaced by
other systems that recreated the relationship of one group at the
bottom to the other group at the top. Some of the mechanisms for
oppressing people in a system of colonialism (as set forth by
Tillman and Tillman) are slavery, sharecropping, dis-
enfranchisement, political control, forced labor, racism, dual labor
and housing markets, and systematic cultural repression. These
mechanisms seldom function alone but as a coherent whole. They
form a system that maintains the domination of the white group
and the oppression of the Black group.

In a speech in 1972 Lerone Bennett commented: "The dark
ghettoes of America are social, political, and above all—economic—
colonies. Their inhabitants are subject people, victims of the greed,
cruelty, insensitivity, guilt, and fear of their masters."

In order to clarify the relationship between Black people in
America and their colonizers, Bennett makes an analogy, comparing
the ghetto with a developing country. The ghetto has a relatively
low per capita income and a high birth rate. Its residents are for the
most part unskilled. Businesses in the Black community do not
have adequate capital or expertise to expand them. The local markets are limited (usually to Black clientele). The ghetto is totally dependent, with only one export—its unskilled labor. The local businesses are owned by white nonresidents. Important jobs in the
ghetto economy are held by white outsiders (teachers, policemen,
postmen). Thus, the Black ghetto is in many ways similar to that of
a typical developing country.

Important in the working of the system is a dual labor and housing market that is linked to the educational system. Each institution
in the society forms an interlocking web so that political and economic domination gives rise to cultural domination, which in turn
reinforces political and economic domination.

Bennett points out that inferior education in ghetto schools hand-
icaps Black workers in the labor market. Blacks are then discrimi-
nated against in employment, and this creates low wages and frequent unemployment. With low incomes, Blacks have difficulty
obtaining good housing. Lack of good education, low level occupations, and exclusion from ownership and control of large enter-
prises prevents Blacks from developing political power; thus they

cannot change basic housing, planning, and educational programs. Each area strengthens the total oppression of Black people.

Under a system of colonialism, the domination of a people is as important as their exploitation because domination is the means by which exploitation can be maintained. Therefore, the educational system must aid in cultural repression and must create a rationale for colonialism.

In a system of colonialism, the colonizer has a dual purpose for educating the colonized. The first is socialization into accepting the value system, history, and culture of the dominant society. The second is education for economic productivity. The oppressed are treated like commodities imbued with skills that are bought and sold on the labor market for the profit of the capitalists.

The educator advocating liberation has parallel purposes for educating the oppressed: education for *struggle* and education for *survival*.

Education for struggle has a consciousness-raising function for Black people, instructing them concerning the following realities:

- who they are
- who the enemy is
- what the enemy is doing to them
- what to struggle for
- what form the struggle must take

Education for struggle must change the kind of Black person produced by the American educational system. Carter G. Woodson (1933) called this system "miseducation," which commits intellectual genocide on Black people and drains potential leadership from the struggle for liberation:

If you control a man's thinking, you do not have to worry about his action. When you determine what a man shall think, you do not have to concern yourself about what he will do. If you make a man feel that he is inferior, you do not have to compel him to accept an inferior status, for he will seek it himself. If you make a man think that he is justly an outcast, you do not have to order him to the back door. He will go without being told; and if there is no back door, his very nature will demand one (pp. 84–85).

Woodson maintains that most Black people who have been educated by the oppressor are not equipped to struggle for liberation until they "recover" from their education. They are taught by the oppressor how to function in the best interest of the system. Often, in this process, they become more oppressor-like than the oppressor.

Paulo Friere (1968) points out that when the oppressed think of liberation, they think of themselves becoming oppressors. Their view is individualistic. Because of their identification with the oppressor, they have no consciousness of themselves as persons or as members of an oppressed class. It is not to become free men that they want agrarian reform, but to acquire land and thus become landowners—or, more precisely, to become bosses over other workers. He gives the example of the peasant who becomes an overseer and becomes more of a tyrant toward his former comrades than the owner himself. This behavior occurs because oppression remains unchanged in his situation. In order to make sure of his job, he must be not only as tough as the owner but more so. Thus, we see that as a result of oppression, the oppressed find in the oppressor their model of "manhood." This situation in the Black community is tragic because miseducated Black people cannot render service to the liberation struggle. Educated into the ways of the system, they become its guardians and are afraid to participate in changing it.

It may be instructive at this point to differentiate between Negro history, white studies, and Black studies. Negro history is an outgrowth of what Patterson (1972) calls *contributionism,* consisting of preserving the forgotten accomplishments of individual Afro-Americans. Negro history implies that the American system is good by conveying the notion that anyone can "make it" who tries. Even though the masses of Black people are suffering, Negro history teaches patience, a belief in tokenism, and the idea that one by one Blacks will achieve liberation.

James Turner (1971) defines traditional American education as tantamount to "white studies." It has functioned to prepare Black people to accept, value, and affirm white society.

White studies is a system of intellectual legitimacy which defines the activities and experiences of white Western people as the universal yardstick of human existence. Black studies challenges this assumption and asserts that white is not now, nor has it ever been either intrinsically right or complete. White students are educated to be the rulers and makers of their society. Blacks are taught to synthesize the experiences and memorize the conclusions of another people. The consequence of such education is that many Blacks, if not most, are inclined to confuse the interest of our people with that of our oppressor; creating a situation where we accept the white people's definitions of the problems they cause for us and the situations they deem acceptable for Black people (p. 12).

Even though Black studies include the preservation of the history and culture of Afro-Americans, its thrust is not the memorization of the names of Black entertainers, scholars, and political figures.

Black studies is a story of *struggle*. Struggle is the key concept. The objective of Black studies is to convey the struggle in which Black people have been engaged against European colonialism throughout history, across the African diaspora. The objective is to recognize the resistance Black people have maintained against this oppression, which has been constant from the time of the African who jumped overboard a slave ship during the Middle Passage to the current marches and protests against cutbacks in social programs.

The forms of Black oppression change with current events. Therefore, a function of Black studies is to enable each generation to identify oppression in its various forms and disguises and to formulate a strategy for struggling against it. Turner (1971) emphasizes the point: "Black education must make students consistently conscious of struggle and commitment. Black studies programs must develop Black youth with a revolutionary sense of identity" (p. 17).

An important issue is how to translate this political ideology into an appropriate educational environment, first for preschool children and later for older children in an alternative school. Packaging seems to be important to Black parents. I was involved in conversations with Black parents as a part of an effort initiated in Atlanta, Georgia, by Patricia Clement, Shirley Franklin, and Janet Douglass to start an alternative school for Black children. Although these parents are politically aware and essentially agree with the analysis of the Black situation outlined in the preceding section, they do not want their children to be harshly indoctrinated in the educative process, nor do they want their children taught to hate white people. They do not necessarily want their children's teachers to wear African clothing and to speak Swahili. They criticize some alternative schools for creating environments that are in some ways as hostile and alien to their experience as that in the white mainstream.

Instead, they express a desire for an educational environment that complements the home and community culture. They want a broadening of the traditional curriculum to include the study and legitimizing of African and Afro-American culture along with the assimilation of skills their children will need to survive in mainstream American culture. They don't want indoctrination; they want inclusion of the Black perspective. They don't want their children bludgeoned with Negro history to the exclusion of the other things they need to learn about the world. These parents want to correct the compartmentalizing of Black people into the Negro History corner of the classroom. They want to see the Black experience integrated into songs, arithmetic problems, science experiments, arts and crafts activities, social studies, and dance forms.

Black parents want the political situation of Black people to be conveyed in the educative process through attention given to helping their children develop an alternative frame of reference, positive self-concepts, a Black identity, and a commitment to their people. This does not mean their children will learn to hate white people. It means they will disdain oppression, domination, exploitation, and repression wherever they see it.

The political ideology of an alternative school will strengthen the commitment and identification of Black children with the group. They will understand that their individual survival is tied to the survival and development of Black people. The thrust of this model will be to reduce individualism and competition, so pervasive in American society.

Pedagogical relevance. The foregoing discussion focused upon the ideology that undergirds correct education for Black children. The Black community has been engaged in a struggle to see their experiences, history, and lifestyles reflected in the education their children receive. However, the second question that must be addressed is the *method* that will be used for the education of Black children. "The tools that are used to destroy men cannot be used for his rehumanization" (Friere 1968, p. 65).

In the preceding chapters of this book, existing research studies have been reviewed in a beginning effort to describe the culture of the Black community and to hypothesize its effects on the learning styles of Black children. Based on this admittedly tenuous foundation, an alternative curricular model will be described that suggests ideas for changing the way Black children are treated in the educative process so that it will be more compatible with the culturally influenced behavioral styles they bring to school.

Academic rigor. The third component of an alternative curricular model is academic rigor. Most Black parents would support teaching Black studies as defined in this book. However, they are equally concerned about companion issues related to the content of their children's education. Black children must be *excellent.* If history has taught any reality to the Afro-American community, it is that Black people have had to excel over white people in every field of endeavor in order to be given an equal opportunity. The white community has created its own rhetoric in opposition to affirmative action programs and has attempted to convey the notion that inept, unqualified Blacks have been given jobs and opportunities at the expense of better qualified whites. However, throughout the Black experience in America, in the name of affirmative action, super-achieving Blacks have been selected as tokens and have been given opportunities available to average whites. The backlash against affirmative action has been caused by such practices. In a *New York Times Magazine* article (October 5, 1980), Carl Gershman, a white man, vice-president of the Social Democrats, USA, engaged in a debate with Black psychologist Dr. Kenneth Clark over affirmative action. Gershman's position was that the Black middle-class is the beneficiary of affirmative action, not the ghetto "under-class." He overlooked the fact that affirmative action is not the design of the Black middle-class; it is the design of the white American system of tokenism. When white universities seek Black students in an effort to integrate their student bodies, they do not seek the "brother on the corner." They recruit Black students from middle-class families, gifted programs, and preparatory schools, who have "white" SAT scores. When the white students encounter these Black students on college campuses and later in corporations, they feel a resentment because the Black students seem to be receiving preferential opportunity. Both the opportunity and the resentment become a double-edged sword for the Black person, who must bear a badge of inferiority because ostensibly he or she is in the setting because of affirmative action. White students are unaware the Black student is there because of achievement that exceeds that of *average* white people.

If white social architects were sincerely interested in targeting affirmative action opportunities toward the "suffering Black masses," they would select people in this strata for their schools and job-training programs. However, they seek the super-achieving Blacks.

Black parents know that Black children will not be able to survive if they are mediocre; therefore, their education must equip them for excellence.

Volumes have been written about the scientific racism implicit in intelligence testing of Black children. Black parents are aware that these tests have figured prominently in the destruction of self-concept and in denials of admission to educational and employment opportunities for Black people. However, at this moment in history, Black psychologists and educators have been unsuccessful in neutralizing the effect of these tests, even by pointing out the flaws in their theory, development, standardization, and interpretation. A curriculum for Black children must imbue Black children with the skills and exposures that are necessary to perform well on such measures.

Curricular Goals

Early-childhood educators commonly accept that preschool environments should be as homelike as possible. However, because many social scientists regard the Black home as pathological, this

Black parents know their children will not be able to survive if they are mediocre. Therefore, their education must equip them for excellence.

principle is often not applied to preschool programs designed for Black children. Every attempt should be made to incorporate key features of the Black child's home into the preschool learning environment. The teachers, as much as possible, should be drawn from the community. The intent is to create a learning environment that complements the culture of the home.

Every attempt should be made to incorporate key features of the home into the learning environment.

The emphasis of this program is to make a child happy and comfortable in *any* preschool. We are more concerned with providing a child with pleasant learning experiences than with preparing him to conform to future school environments, facilitating his adjustment to the classroom without having to be overly concerned about whether he will adjust later when he enters public school. In other words, our primary goal is to help the child enjoy learning—not simply to prepare him or her for the public schools. If we can demonstrate the effectiveness of this model, we may be able to make an impact on educational programs for older children.

The philosophy of this model is that the purpose of preschool education is to provide the child with planned group experiences that will enrich his background and enhance his or her readiness for formal instruction in the elementary school. The function of early education is not to push the content of the first grade downward into earlier and earlier age levels. Therefore, the overall orientation will be to expose children to a wide range of experiences. The curriculum will be balanced so that Afro-American culture is

The teachers, as much as possible, should be drawn from the community.

explored and legitimated at the same time that the children are taught about Euro-American and other cultures. Although the curriculum content will be broad, basic areas will be emphasized in this model:

1. *Language/communication skills.* Language-related skills are critical in the education of children. A high correlation exists between elementary school reading achievement test scores and standardized college admissions tests. This correlation suggests that a huge proportion of what is being measured in "intelligence" and "achievement" tests are language/communication skills.

Black children have distinctive difficulties in mastering standard English and in achieving reading proficiency. Therefore, speaking, listening, labeling, storytelling, chanting, imitating, and reciting will be encouraged.

Educators must be sensitive to the many as yet unidentified ways in which Black children are "turned off" and "pushed out" of school.

2. *Mathematical concepts.* Black children are able to master a wide range of mathematical skills in their everyday lives (like computing baseball batting averages), but they have difficulty demonstrating their skills in the classroom. Therefore, emphasis will be placed upon developing mathematical proficiency in this model program.

3. *Positive self-concept and positive attitude toward learning and school.* This affective goal is included as an overall curricular emphasis because children should not be imbued with cognitive skills at the expense of a consideration for the way they feel about themselves, the teacher, learning, and the school. Educators must be sensitive to the many as yet unidentified ways in which Black children are "turned off" and "pushed out" of school.

Equally important as achievement test scores is providing children with success experiences, enabling them to be self-motivating and to establish a life-long love of learning.

4. *Afro-American studies.* Afro-American studies is a focal point and also will be integrated throughout the curriculum of this model. Every opportunity will be used to acquaint the children with the culture, cosmology, history, and perspective of Africans of the diaspora. As a result of this exposure, the children should have more information about Black culture and increased pride in their racial heritage.

The curriculum will include countless topics and information drawn from numerous disciplines that will be presented on the level of the child. The curriculum will include science, art, music, creative movement, geography, nutrition, history, social studies, economics, literature, and philosophy. However, these areas of the curriculum will be taught in an integrated manner through field trips, speakers, movies, units, and incidental learning.

Features of the Model

1. *High affective support.* The classroom will have a high adult-child ratio, small-group learning, peer tutoring, and heterogeneous grouping (family style). The children will be grouped on a rotating basis so that they work with children of their own age; with older and younger children; and with those who have more, less, and similar abilities. Frequent touching, lap-sitting, holding hands, and hugging will be encouraged.

2. *Self-concept development.* Children's self-confidence will be fostered through frequent compliments, praise, display of work, performances, open houses, and frequent success experiences. Care will be taken that display of children's work (all children, not just a few) will exceed display of teacher's work (art, bulletin boards).

3. *Creative expression.* Opportunities for all types of creative expression will permeate the curriculum. The visual, dramatic, and musical arts will be encouraged.

4. *Arts and crafts.* The children will be involved in arts and crafts, with emphasis on those that are a part of African and Afro-American culture.

5. *Activities.* Frequent opportunities will be provided for physical release and for the children to teach themselves through play. Movement activities will be used in the learning process. Dance and creative movement will be taught. The classroom will be organized to permit maximum child movement, with as much self-direction as is practical.

6. *African culture.* The children will be exposed to aspects of African culture appropriate to their level of understanding—foods, geography, fashions, music, instruments, songs, poetry, names, history, and art.

Self-confidence is fostered through frequent compliments and praise.

7. *Afro-American culture.* The children will learn about Afro-American culture—foods, music, folklore, art, literature, and history.

8. *Extracurricular experiences.* Numerous experiences will be planned to broaden the horizons of the children. They will be exposed to a variety of foods. However, creative care will be taken to incorporate foods from Afro-American culture into the curriculum so that the children will feel comfortable in the "nutritional environment." Frequent field trips will be planned. A variety of "teachers" from the community as well as parents and grandparents will be regularly brought into the classroom to teach special skills.

9. *Holidays.* Attention will be given to the politics of holidays, particularly as they affect the history of Black and other oppressed people in America. For example, if Thanksgiving is discussed, it will not be a celebration of the point of view of the "pilgrims." It will be an exploration of the situation of Native Americans, Afro-Americans, and the European colonizers. The same principle will apply to the Fourth of July. Celebrations and commemorations will revolve around events and historical figures pivotal in the Afro-American liberation struggle.

Teaching Strategies

1. *Body language.* Black children are proficient in nonverbal communication. Teachers should be sensitive in their use of gestures, eye-contact, and other nonverbal cues.

2. *Standard English.* Standard English should be modeled, and children's speech should be informally corrected. This modeling and correcting are very important in early childhood because if a child doesn't "hear" certain sounds and develop the ability to reproduce them early in life, it becomes more difficult to change speech patterns later. More research is needed in the instructional needs of Black English speakers; however, one fact is clear: speaking standard English is a skill needed by Black children for upward mobility in American society and should be taught in early childhood. At no time should baby talk be spoken. The teachers should speak in complete sentences and should encourage the children to do so.

3. *Equal talking time.* Teacher "talk" should be regulated to the approximate amount of child talk. Laura Lein found in her study of Black migrant children that the children spoke more frequently and used more complex sentences outside of school with peers and parents. This phenomenon occurred because the peers and parents talked about the same amount as the children, who spoke least to the teacher in school, seemingly because the teacher talked a greater proportion of the time.

The teacher should encourage the children to talk conversationally, in recitation, and creatively.

4. *Group learning.* An emphasis should be made on small group learning and hands-on contact with the teacher. When a child is not working with an adult, he or she should be learning with peers.

5. *A variety of learning activities.* Children should be taught with a varied format for learning activities—movement, games, music, prose, poetry.

6. *Music in the classroom.* Afro-American music should permeate the curriculum. Jazz, rhythm and blues, and disco music should be played (whenever it is practical) frequently throughout the day. Black children are exposed to music in their homes, and it is relaxing to them. Some teachers have reported that discipline problems decreased and productivity increased when music was played in classrooms with Black children. The children should not only be exposed to the music but also should be taught about the artists.

Equipment and Materials

1. *Play equipment.* Many research studies have indicated that Black children are more physically precocious than white children, also

Children should be taught with a variety of formats.

that physical activity is encouraged in Afro-American culture. Therefore, the children in the preschools will be given the opportunity to develop their large muscles. Indoor and outdoor play equipment will be selected with that goal in mind.

2. *Learning materials.* Open-ended learning materials will be selected: clay, water play, sandboxes, socio-dramatic play props (dress-up clothes, fabric for creative wrapping). Care should be taken to avoid flooding the classroom with toys, particularly those that are structured and gadgetlike. Learning games should be chosen that the children can play together, such as those that teach mathematical concepts.

The Teacher
The teacher of this model curriculum should be someone who believes in the ideology of the school. Ideally, this person should live in the community and share the culture of the children. It is important that the teacher has achieved the "duality of socialization" that is the goal for Black children. She or he should share, understand, and participate in Black culture. On the other hand, the teacher should have assimilated enough of mainstream culture to be able to model behaviors that will enable the children to become upwardly mobile. This is a delicate balance to achieve, but it is one that most Black parents strive for in their child-rearing. Black people disdain members of the group who look down upon their fellows and seek to escape from their heritage. But they admire those who are able to function *as a Black person* in mainstream positions of responsibility. The teacher of this curriculum should understand that distinction and exhibit that ability.

The teacher should be formally trained in child development, learning theory, early childhood education methods and materials, early childhood education curriculum, and Afro-American studies. She or he should engage in constant study of the child, the family, and the community in order to create a dynamic curriculum constantly infused with new insight into the educational process.

The teacher must understand and respect Black culture and should respect and work well with parents, regarding them as partners in educating the child. She or he should provide opportunities for parents to assist in assessing and evaluating the strengths, weaknesses, and progress of their children.

Discipline
Management of the behavior of Black children in the classroom is a concern of both Black and white teachers. However, little systematic research exists to provide insight into the problem. There-

Ideally the teacher should share the culture of the children.

fore, Black children, particularly males, are regarded as unruly, aggressive, and difficult to manage.

As a beginning point in reconceptualizing the behavior management of Black children, a teacher must acknowledge that there are no physical developmental norms for Black children. It is generally assumed that the physical development of all children conforms to the pattern identified for white children. In those instances where Black children have been identified as more active than white children, they have been labeled hyperactive. As we mentioned earlier, a disproportionate number of Black children have been given this label. More study is needed about the ways in which Black children develop physically and about the amount of freedom they are given at home to move and to play.

Many of the discipline problems teachers experience with Black children may be caused because the children are expected to conform to a white behavioral model. Teachers can avoid behavioral problems by providing active periods when the children can expend excess energy and rest periods when they become tired and irritable. Many children do not receive enough rest at night, and their resultant fatigue is reflected in behavioral problems in the classroom.

If a teacher finds that the children are not getting enough sleep, she or he can bring it to the attention of the parents and can stress the need for enforced bedtimes. Many parents of Black preschool children are very young. They sometimes feel that they are being lenient and kind to the children by permitting them to stay up late with adults, such permission often offered as a reward for good behavior (for example to allow watching a favorite television program). However, lack of sleep places a hardship on children, who must arise early and play and learn very actively at day-care centers, where many remain for ten to twelve hours a day.

If a teacher is unable to convince the parents to arrange for more rest at home, she or he should plan for periods of rest throughout the day.

Nutrition is another important area that affects behavior. Many children in lower-income communities may not have malnutrition, but they may be less well-nourished than their more advantaged counterparts. Eating junk foods and foods that are loaded with sugar and carbohydrates can create behavioral problems. The teacher can have a nutritionist speak at parent meetings about the importance of providing a balanced diet for young children. But in addition, the *children* should be taught directly about the importance of making good choices in foods. Black children are usually independent at an early age and have a fair amount of choice in what they

Eating junk foods and foods that are loaded with sugar and carbohydrates can create behavioral problems.

eat. It is important, then, that the preschool help them develop wise preferences (fruit over candy, for example). The children can be taught to report what they ate the previous day as a part of their learning activities so that the teacher can obtain a profile of the dietary habits of the children.

Masculinity

I mentioned earlier I had hypothesized that the Black community projects a different model of masculinity from that of the Euro-American culture. Blacks have a kind of raunchy macho best illustrated by sports figures like Muhammad Ali and Walt Frazier. Black males perfect a special walk, place value on being "cool" (unflappable), cultivate distinctive handshakes and slang, share common manhood rites (playing the dozens, woofing, fighting, and vying for sports prowess), and socialize each other into characteristic approaches toward authority figures and women. They actually share a subculture within the Black community.

Traditional classrooms are generally oriented toward feminine values. Teachers are disproportionately female, and the behaviors tolerated and encouraged are those that are more natural for girls. White males also often come into conflict in the traditional classroom, but Black males have the most difficult adjustment. The hier-

Black communities project a different model of masculinity from that of the Euro-American culture.

archy of comfort in traditional classrooms is as follows: white females, Black females, white males, and Black males.

The teacher in a model classroom would be sensitive to many ways in which Black maleness is rejected in traditional classrooms. For example, when Black male children volley verbally in an aggressive, threatening manner, some teachers who don't understand Black culture may interpret their behavior as "fighting" when actually they are "woofing," a verbal ritual that relieves tension in lieu of a fight.

Thomas Kochman discusses this Black cultural ritual in a paper entitled " 'Fighting Words': Black and White." He concludes that whites essentially believe that hostile words and violent acts are different forms of the *same* thing, while Blacks generally conceive them to be different things. Kochman describes woofing as a ritual wherein anger and hostility can be sustained at the verbal level without violence necessarily resulting. He also says that a *dramatic* dimension of woofing renders it as acting, so that it functions as play. Through woofing, a player can maintain an image of being fearless and tough with the hope that once that image is achieved, he won't have to prove it.

Kochman further says that within the playful context of speech events such as woofing, signifying, sounding, and playing the dozens, a culturally determined point indicates when the fight *begins* or when someone signals that he intends to fight. That signal is a *provocative movement* within the context of an angry confrontation. Kochman quotes an example from a description provided by one of his students:

If two guys are talkin' loud and then one or the other starts to reduce the distance between them, that's a sign because it's important to get in the first blow. Or if a guy puts his hand in his pocket and that's not part of his normal stance, then you watch for that—he might be reaching for a knife. But if they're just talkin'—doesn't matter how loud it gets—then you got nothin' to worry about (p. 36).

This is only one example of the numerous ways in which male children run into conflict with authority figures because their culture is diametrically opposed to the Euro-American and feminine culture of the schools. Other conflicts that should be studied are the following:

- Often white teachers regard the special walk of the Black males as sassy.
- Because of the emphasis upon sports and physical activity in the Black community, it may be difficult for Black male children to sit quietly for long periods of time.
- In many instances, white teachers are unable to discipline Black children because they do not "connect" culturally; the teachers do not behave as Black children expect authority figures to behave. White social scientists have interpreted the way Black mothers reprimand their children as harsh. However, recent interpretations of this cultural style (Piestrup 1974, Baumrind 1972) have suggested that the *children* do not regard the interchange to be as harsh as do the white observers. In fact, Piestrup regards the threats and harsh reprimands as bordering on play.

It seems that when white teachers practice the disciplinary techniques they are taught in college, Black children "run over" them. However, because Black teachers emerge from a culture common to Black students, Black teachers are better able to discipline Black children. More research is needed to sharpen the analysis of this phenomenon.

In the final analysis, says James Young (Norment 1981), discipline is self-management. The goal of the teacher is to structure the classroom environment in such a way as to provide minimal conflict and maximum opportunity for the child to manage himself or herself. Particularly with preschool children, where numerous disciplinary problems exist, the teacher should examine the schedule, the fatigue level of the children, the difficulty or monotony of the activities, and the nutrition or health of the children as first steps in diagnosing the problem. The teacher should be sure that classroom rules are realistic and flexible and that they are understood by the children.

Gloria Powell, a child psychiatrist at the University of California at the Los Angeles Center for Health Services emphasizes the importance of deciding on basic rules of conduct for children and communicating these rules clearly and consistently: disciplining in the same manner each time a rule is broken, and complimenting and praising a child when he has followed the rules. (Norment 1981).

Evaluation

This model should be closely monitored to assess the achievement of affective and cognitive goals. For decades Black teachers and educational institutions have distinguished themselves in educating Black people. However, they could document their effectiveness only by pointing with pride to outstanding individuals their institutions produced. It is time now for Black schools to collect data to monitor the progress of their students. One purpose for these data is to revise the curriculum and methodology as pupil outcomes become known. The other purpose is to provide ongoing documentation on the results of the program for public relations reasons and for aiding development efforts.

Evaluation is a valuable tool for merging innovation and tradition. Even though a fundamental objection exists to the philosophy and design of intelligence tests, standardized inventories can be used to obtain baseline information on language and cognitive achievement. I repeat the importance of utilizing some mainstream assessment measures to be used continually to measure children throughout their educational careers. However, it is also important to supplement those measures with observations, anecdotal notes, examples of work, checklists, and other naturalistic measures.

It is also important to include parents and peers as evaluators. Opportunities should be provided for parents to engage in systematic observation at home and in the classroom, if possible. Techniques such as sociograms and checklists should be used for children to evaluate each other. Asa Hilliard (1976) demonstrated how to elicit information from parents and peers to identify giftedness among Black children.

Parental Involvement

Parental involvement programs for a preschool that services Black lower-income children need rethinking. In some 'poverty' programs, parents have been badgered by "parental involvement." In too many instances, parental involvement has meant attending meetings. Parents have been labeled uninterested in their children if attendance at meetings is not high.

It is not the intent of this section to outline a parental involvement program; some excellent books perform that function (Nedler and McAfee 1979, for example). However, a few suggestions will be made here to guide the design of a parental involvement component to complement the curriculum of the model school.

Educators must recognize at the outset that a large proportion of parents of lower-income preschool Black children are young (teenaged to early adulthood), and many are single females. They are parents at a turbulent period in their lives. Many are in school and in job-training programs that place a great burden on their time and energy. Being single requires a different kind of energy than being married. A great amount of unpredictability characterizes lower-income life. For example, often people must depend upon time-consuming public transportation. A greater interdependence among family members places unexpected demands on their time. More incidence of illness exists because of poor nutrition and medical care. Setbacks are caused by their living in high-crime areas.

Therefore, parental involvement programs designed with the suburban housewife in mind are inappropriate for most Black preschool programs. Input must come from parents for designing the content of educational seminars and for scheduling activities. Offering seminars on applying make-up or preparing for a job interview may seem to be unrelated to the school and the child; in fact, it intersects with the interests of the parent. Over a period of time, a parent will give more to the school and the child when more of his or her needs have been met.

The parental-involvement program must reflect a balanced view of the Black lower-income family. The teacher must be able to conceptualize the adaptive aspects of the family as interpreted by the "strengths of Black families" school. On the other hand, poverty must not be romanticized. At the same time that lower-income Blacks participate in the joy of Black life, they are also plagued by crime, poor health, poor housing, and limited opportunities for upward mobility.

Most Black lower-income parents have high aspirations for themselves and their children. However, often they are not in the flow of information that enables them to realize those aspirations. Therefore, a balanced parental involvement program should share information with the parents that will assist them in their struggle for survival and achievement. In summary, a parental involvement program should neither slander nor romanticize the parents. Their strengths should be extended and their input solicited, but they should also receive needed assistance and information.

An educational component for parents should be a part of this model program. Seminars should be offered in child development and learning theory so that parents and teachers can complement each other's efforts. Important also are seminars in African and Afro-American studies for parents. Because Black studies are not widely taught in educational institutions, parents must study Black culture so that they can extend their children's learning experiences at home and share the joy of discovering their heritage.

Some educators expect parents to be drawn to this model program because they agree with its basic thrust. However, as this school develops, its ideology will continue to evolve. Therefore, the educational staff should have a dialogue with parents about ideological issues, such as the celebration of holidays. The staff should achieve a balance between sharing with parents the thinking that undergirds the political analysis of this model and including them in the decision-making process.

The conclusion of this book should be regarded as a commencement. We who share the spirituality of the Black experience know it and feel it. We can see the expression of Black culture in the behavioral styles of Black children. However, more research is needed to enable us to build bridges between the culture of the home and the school.

Carter G. Woodson (1933), the Father of Negro History, had infinite faith in the ability of educators to effect change that would benefit the Black community, as evidenced in these words:

Can you expect teachers to revolutionize the social order for the good of the community? Indeed we must expect this very thing. The educational system of a country is worthless unless it accomplishes this task. Men of scholarship, and consequently of prophetic insight, must show us the right way and lead us unto the light which shines brighter and brighter (p. 145).

Epilogue

Black children are educationally at risk. There is an achievement gap between Black and white children in the schools of this nation. A recent report by the National Alliance of Black School Educators (NABSE) (1984) tells us that nearly 28 percent of Afro-American high school students drop out before graduation. This figure approaches 50 percent in some large cities. For those who are in school, average achievement on standardized tests is two or more grade levels below the average for Euro-American students. Even though Blacks compose only slightly more than 10 percent of the population, they make up 40 percent of the educable mentally retarded population (p. 18).

An examination of the achievement statistics of a midwest surburban school district that has been listed as one of the top school systems in the country documents this disparity between Black and white achievement (Jefferson, 1985). The school system is racially integrated; of the 1,450 high school students, 40 percent are Black and 60 percent are white. At every grade level, Blacks scored significantly lower than whites on the Stanford Achievement Test, which is used nationally to measure reading and mathematics skills. Of Black students between the seventh and eleventh grades, 78.2 percent scored *below* the average on the reading test, while 89 percent of white students scored *above* the average. Math scores were equally low; 79.7 percent of Blacks scored below the average and 87 percent of whites scored above the average.

Classroom performance paralleled test scores. In the class of 1985, 51 percent of Black eleventh-grade males and 55 percent of Black females had grade point averages below 1.99. In contrast, only 20 percent of white males and 9 percent of white females had grade point averages below 1.99. Furthermore, a mere 10 percent of Black students had grade point averages at or above 3.00, whereas 34 percent of white females and 37 percent of white males had grade point averages above 3.00. Officials of this school system point out that these scores reflect a trend found in other school systems throughout the country.

NABSE (1984) points out that the difficulties Black children are experiencing in elementary and secondary schools are reflected in an erosion of achievement in higher education. "African Americans represent about 13.5 percent of the college age population (18–24 years). But African-American students represented only 9.1 percent of the Associate degrees, 6.5 percent of the Bachelors, 6.4 percent of the Masters, and 3.9 percent of the Doctorates, and 4.1 percent of the first professional degrees in 1980. African-American participation in graduate and professional education remains exceptionally low and, in recent years the situation has actually deteriorated" (p. 20).

This report states that one third of Black students are enrolled in community colleges in programs that do not necessarily give credits toward a baccalaureate degree. We also find that, while about 75 percent of all white high school seniors go on to college, only about 20 percent of Black seniors do so. Further, only about 12 percent of the Black students who begin higher education complete college and only 4 percent complete a graduate program.

The education of white children is relatively more successful than that of Black children because the schools are designed for white education. As Hakim Rashid (1981) has stated, "children from non-European lower socioeconomic status cultural groups are at a disadvantage in the schools because the American education system has evolved out of a European philosophical, theoretical, and pedagogical context" (p. 57).

W. E. B. DuBois (1903) described the Black person in America as having two warring souls. On the one hand, Black people are the product of their African-American heritage and culture. On the other hand, they are shaped by the demands of Euro-American culture. Unfortunately, the Euro-American influence has been emphasized to the exclusion of the African influence. Despite the pressure of four hundred years in America, African Americans have not melted into the pot. Rashid (1981) has pointed out that, "the cultural and biological history of African-Americans has resulted in an 'essentially African' group of people who must function in 'essentially' European schools" (p. 58).

The thesis of this book is to offer an alternative approach to conceptualizing the behavioral styles of Black children and to lay the foundation for devising educational strategies that complement Black culture. It is a radical departure from the pathology model of the past two decades.

During the 1960s, when the compensatory education programs were designed, comparative research was conducted with middle-class white children and lower-income Black children. This practice created an image of the Black child as poor, the product of a disorganized family, and essentially to blame for his own low achievement at school. One can only surmise in examining this model that there are no middle-class or even working-class Black children who have survived and become upwardly mobile against incredible odds, because such a child and family are not visible in the social science literature.

This tendency to contrast white middle-class culture with Black lower-class culture in the social science literature has served, much like the depiction of Blacks on television, to create an image that all whites are middle class and all Blacks are under class. An example of this is the depiction of Blacks as the prototypical welfare recipients, when in fact there are more whites than Blacks on welfare (Hill, 1981, p. 37).

White social scientists engage in a type of chauvinistic ethnocentrism that perpetuates an image of normality in describing white children and of pathology in describing Black children. Dr. Anna Grant, chairperson of the sociology department at Morehouse College, has pointed out that white social scientists use harsh terms when describing a phenomenon that affects Blacks and more neutral terms when discussing middle-class whites. During the 1950s, when Blacks were the principal drug users, they were defined as drug addicts. Now that drug use is pervasive in the white middle class, we see terms like "drug culture," "chemical dependency," "substance abuse." Out-of-wedlock births were defined as illegitimate when it was thought that they occurred largely among Blacks. As it has been acknowledged that such births are common in the white middle-class community as well, terms such as "single motherhood," "single-parent lifestyle," and even "liberated babies" have replaced the more pejorative ones. Venereal disease, VD, has been renamed STD, socially transmitted disease. Black children who skip school are truants, but upper middle-class white children might have "school phobia" and require treatment. While poor Black children who do not perform well in school are likely to be moved into classes for the mentally retarded, children from white upper-income families who perform poorly are designated "underachievers," in need of special counseling and educational services. We define and pinpoint their disabilities with diagnoses like dyslexia, and we create categories like "learning disability" to differentiate their problems.

However, the scientific misrepresentation of Black children does not end with behavior. Black children are defined in white terms because white children are considered by psychologists to represent the norm. That criterion for normality pervades the description of psychomotor skills as well as cognitive skills. Psychologists have developed a language and set of standards with which we describe children from diverse ethnic groups using a white frame of reference. For example, white social scientists have amassed data such as the Gesell Scales, which describe how white children grow and develop physically. Their characteristics are set forth in child development textbooks as uniformly applicable to all children. This practice persists even though there is a body of data that documents differences in performance by African-American and African children on sensorimotor tasks (Geber, 1958) as well as differences in the ways in which Black children use their bodies (Guttentag, 1972). There is a body of research (Geber, 1958) that suggests that Black children as infants are more advanced in sensorimotor skills than white infants. But we don't therefore say that white children are developmentally delayed at birth, we say that Black children are precocious; thus the notion of white normality is maintained.

When Black children do not approximate the norms for white children, they are regarded as deficient, deviant, or pathological, even when they exceed white children in some dimension. For example, Black children are disproportionately labeled hyperactive because they exhibit different psychomotor skills and needs than do white children. Even though the term "cultural difference" was introduced into the social science literature in the 1970s, it has remained essentially a cliché. "Cultural difference" has been a superficial acknowledgment of Black culture, but it has never been developed as a construct. This book has been designed to put meat on the bones of "cultural difference."

My thesis has met with numerous reactions as I have discussed these issues with teachers throughout the United States. From these reactions some observations can be drawn:

1. There seems to be a fundamental lack of awareness by white teachers that there is a documented achievement gap between Black and white students. They seem not to know the extent of the problem, and they underestimate the relationship between poor performance in school and functional illiteracy, unemployment, drug abuse, poverty, and incarceration.

2. There is a reticence to accede that, given the severity of the problem, it is legitimate to study and to treat the educational difficulties of Black children as a category. There is a tendency to argue instead that Black children's needs can be addressed along with those of other poor children—the disadvantaged—or that they can be grouped with others in a multicultural category. An attempt is made to erode the thesis of a distinctive African-American culture by pointing to isolated traits that culture shares with ethnic heritages. In general, there is an urge to subsume Black children into other less applicable categories. White teachers overlook the remarkable success of historically Black colleges in educating Black

students by tailoring the educational process to meet their needs. Unfortunately, even though we have the products to point to, there has not yet been enough documentation of the process.

3. Many white teachers do not want to acknowledge the historical and contemporary reality of Black oppression. I have heard statements such as, "I am tired of carrying the burden of the past four hundred years on my back." Just as there is a current unwillingness to support affirmative action in employment, there is little inclination in the public mind to acknowledge the effect of racism and discrimination on Black children's performance in school and to invest resources in repairing the damage.

4. There is a nonrecognition of the ways in which politically powerful white parents can manipulate the educational system to protect and secure advantages for their children, creating for them a pattern of safety nets. The advantages of this in boosting the educational and occupational achievements of white middle-class children is ignored. The majority of Black children not only do not have the systemic protection provided for white middle-class children but also must suffer the deleterious effects of racism.

The system of safety nets was very clear to me because I grew up in a middle-class family yet most of my friends and schoolmates were from lower-class families. My friends did not enjoy the courtesies extended to me, the protection my parents could give me because they had political savvy and were well-respected in the community. I saw in stark relief the difference between life for the masses of Black people and the life I was leading.

5. Because there is so little firsthand contact between the races and across social classes, images projected by the mass media play a large role in shaping people's attitudes toward the genesis of social problems and solutions.

It is my intent in this epilogue to address some of the reactions to my work, to fine-tune my thesis that Black culture is coherent and should be considered in the educational process, and to create a framework for moving beyond the lip service being paid cultural difference to the conceptualizing of classroom practices to complement these cultural differences.

The Black community has persistently been in the vanguard in the struggle for multicultural education because of the uniqueness of their biological and cultural history in America. Often the response to Black demands is to recite the atrocities of the Holocaust, which occurred in Europe in the 1930s and 1940s, or otherwise to minimize the uniqueness and severity of the treatment of Africans throughout North and South America.

First of all, every other ethnic group that emigrated to America came seeking a better life. Africans were forcibly brought here and were subjected to brutal slavery. Even when slavery ended, oppression in various forms continued for African Americans.

African Americans also suffered as an ethnic group because of their visibility and inability to "melt" readily in "the pot." Other ethnic groups could blend into the American mainstream after one generation. As pointed out earlier (pp. 26–27), Havighurst's work suggests that certain ethnic groups—those of northern European heritage, European Americans, Jews, Asians—are better able to be assimilated into the mainstream. Other groups, such as those of southern European descent, Spanish-speaking groups, and African Americans, are at greater risk in moving into mainstream institutions such as the schools and the workplace.

Lieberman (1981) has pointed out that even though other nonwhite ethnic groups have suffered oppression in America, the measures employed in response to them and the consequences suffered by them were not as severe as they were for Blacks. For example, when Americans perceived a threat in the number of Asian immigrants, immigration laws were changed to control the number of Asians entering the country. Similarly, Native Americans were relocated and restricted to reservations. Whereas the numbers of these nonwhites were restricted and their movements controlled, Black immigration was forced and a comprehensive system of slavery was instituted that was expected to exist indefinitely.

A central thesis of this book is that one explanation for the difficulties Black children experience in school may be their participation in a culture that is very different from the culture which designed the school. The book is intended to lay a foundation for delineating this culture and for identifying those points of mismatch between it and Euro-American culture that may have educational consequences for Black children. I locate myself clearly among the theorists who trace the genesis of Black culture to the African heritage, but there are other theories. This has generated a great deal of discussion, because the evidence supporting each theory is inconclusive.

It may be useful here to reexamine the theories that have been postulated to explain Black culture.

Theories of Black Culture

Amuzie Chimezie (1984) offers a useful review of various ways of conceptualizing Black culture. He believes the theorists can be divided broadly into two categories, affirmative and negative. Affirmative theorists support the view that there is a distinctive Black culture, even though they differ in the degree to which they think it can be traced to the African heritage. Negative theorists deny the existence of a distinctive Black culture. They attribute any differences between Blacks and whites to differences in class position, degree of poverty, and attendant social pathologies. Let us examine the groups within these categories more closely. The affirmative theories comprise four groups: the African heritage theory, the affirmative New World–experience theory, biculturation theory, and the eclectic theory.

The African Heritage Theory

This theory takes the view that Afro-American culture is distinct from white Euro-American culture and that the vast majority of the distinguishing characteristics are traceable to elements of African culture retained by African slaves in America. The theory acknowledges that many of the cultural artifacts have been modified out of easy recognition, however, a careful scientific comparison with African culture reveals in them the roots of Afro-American culture (Chimezie, p. 217).

The African heritage theory is based principally upon three facts:

First, many of the distinctive cultural elements involved are generally not characteristic of white American Euro-centric culture (e.g., the extended family and Brer Rabbit stories). Second, they are found among virtually all Afro-centric communities in the New World, especially in the Caribbean. Third, those elements still characterize African culture today, especially West Africa, from where most of the Africans were captured for enslavement. The widespread presence of these distinctive cultural elements in the Afro-centric world (in Africa and diaspora) is one of the most persuasive arguments used by the proponents of the African-heritage theory of Black culture (e.g. Herskovits, 1958) (p. 217).

Africanisms abound in Black culture in the United States. For example, Black dialect, including South Carolina Gullah, has been identified as originating from aspects of African language retained by enslaved Africans. Other examples are Black folklore, aspects of Black childrearing, Black music, and Black religious expressions.

Affirmative New World–Experience Theory

This model affirms the existence of a distinctive Black culture but unlike the African heritage theory, explains that distinctiveness in terms of the experience of Blacks in America. Instead of explaining Black cultural elements in terms of African traditions, it searches for explanations in Black experiences in America. A New World–experience theorist of Black culture such as V. P. Franklin (1984), for example, traces Blacks' high valuation of the cultural values of freedom, resistance, education, and self-determination directly to their experiences under slavery and in post–Civil War America.

Biculturation Theory

This theory views Black culture as composed of Black and white elements. Charles A. Valentine (1971) describes Blacks as being individually and collectively "bicultural." He argues that Blacks are socialized equally in Afro-American and Euro-American culture. A major point of disagreement among proponents of this theory is whether both cultures are of equal importance to Blacks (and whites). Robert Staples (1976) proposes that some of the values of Euro-American culture are antithetical to the Black value system, and he doubts that they are of equal importance to Blacks, as Valentine suggests.

The Eclectic View

The eclectic view of Black culture also recognizes a distinctive Black culture and attempts to identify the salient factors that are theoretically responsible for its cultural elements. It sees some aspects of Black culture as African retentions and others as arising from the American experience. Chimezie states further: "[The eclectic view] realizes that many various factors have influenced and affected Black ways of life and accordingly recognizes those factors. Some of the factors in Black culture recognized in this view include but are not limited to Africa, Christianity, white supremacy and oppression, relative poverty, lower-class status, and contact with other groups in the American society" (p. 219).

The eclectic view encompasses virtually all of the current theories without making a commitment to any one of them.

Negative theories of Black culture are those that deny the existence of a distinctive Black culture. This category includes theories that deny the existence of cultural differences between Blacks and whites. Any differences that exist are attributed not to culture but to pathological responses by Blacks to poverty or white cultural practices (cultural imitation). Differences between Blacks and whites are explained in terms of oppression, poverty, and social class. Negativists de-emphasize an analysis that calls attention to Blacks' African heritage, innovativeness, and cultural integrity (p. 219).

The theories in this category are negative New World–experience theory, the lower-class theory, and the pathology theory.

Negative New World–Experience Theory

This theory denies Black cultural distinctiveness and attributes any observable Black-white cultural differences essentially to an inability of Blacks to master white culture. Unlike the affirmative New World–experience theory, it uses the New World–experience to *explain away* Black cultural distinctiveness. Chimezie sets forth two factors that seem to underlie some of the affirmative and negative New World–experience theories of Black culture: white ethnocentrism and Black rejection of Africa. He states that when Europeans and Euro-Americans were imperialistically destroying the cultures of other societies in the world, a notion emerged that "inferior," or nonliterate, cultures could not survive when brought into contact with "superior," white cultures (p. 219).

He states further that many of the attempts by whites at the beginning of the twentieth century to explain the Black culture of that time were New World–experience theories. They defined Black cultural characteristics as unsuccessful attempts to master Euro-American culture rather than as demonstrations of the resiliency of African traditions.

Another component of the New World theory is Black nonidentification with Africa. Chimezie's analysis of this phenomenon is that "this nonidentification was a function of the disparagement of Africa in both the popular culture and scholarly writings. For example, Africans were characterized as follows: savage (uncivilized), heathenish (non-Christian), 'real' black, 'oversexed,' bestial, related to apes, polygamous, lustful and immoral" (p. 220).

According to Chimezie and Johnson (1978), E. Franklin Frazier seemed to hold the view that the culture of Blacks is really white culture. However, Chimezie attempts to place Frazier's statements in the context of the time in which he wrote: First, Frazier presumably identified with white culture. Second, he implies that there is virtually nothing positive in Black culture and nothing worth preserving, therefore, to him the adoption of white cultural norms was the only way for Blacks to go. Third and probably most compelling, Frazier "began his writings about Blacks in the 1930s, when it was necessary to refute the racist theory that Black cultural difference from whites was a sign of Black inferiority and that the inferiority was a function of race and genes" (p. 223).

The Lower-Class Theory

This theory proposes that Blacks are not really culturally different from whites and that what is regarded as Black culture is really lower-class culture caused by poverty. It is supported by reference to the similarities between some aspects of Black culture and of lower-class white culture. Chimezie names Frazier, John Scanzoni, Oscar Lewis, and Bennett Berger as theorists who perceive Black culture as lower-class, nonethnic culture. These theorists essentially attribute any differences between Black and white family structures to discrimination and differential access to opportunity. They deny that Blacks have a valid ethnic culture that is not a function of poverty (p. 224).

Chimezie feels that this theory is particularly appealing to upwardly mobile Blacks who hasten to distance themselves from the masses of Black people, that it is appealing to Blacks who are trying to be white because it supports their assertion that only lower-class Blacks are different, "that Blacks have the capacity to become white ('civilized'), and that those Blacks who have had the opportunity (middle-class) have become white, and that, given the same opportunity, the rest would be acculturated."

Chimezie also believes that this theory is attractive to opponents of Black Studies or any kind of affirmative treatment of Blacks educationally or culturally. If they could reduce Black-white tensions in this country to class conflict, then it would be easier to destroy Blacks culturally (since approximately one-third belong to the lower class), without being accused of ethnic or racial genocide. Chimezie states, "Contemporary conscience seems to tolerate interclass oppression better than interracial or interethnic oppression. . . . This theory would be welcome since the dominant group would then not have to make adjustments for Blacks any more than they have to make for poor lower-class whites" (p. 224).

A consequence of the lower-class theory that is especially pertinent to this book is the definition of Black children as "culturally deprived" because they are deprived of white cultural experiences. The inference is that they have not been raised in the "right" (read "white") cultural context. Pressure from the Black community has caused awareness of cultural differences to evolve into recognition of cultural difference. However, as noted earlier, we have yet to give programmatic substance to this concept in the same way that the cultural deprivation thesis was institutionalized in compensatory education programs.

The Pathology Theory

This theory holds that Black culture is a sick or diseased version of white culture. The pathological theorist looks at Black culture and sees promiscuity and alcoholism. He uses terms such as "disorganized," "fatalistic," "immoral," "role confusion," "illiterate," "promiscuous," and so forth. Chimezie cites Daniel P. Moynihan (1965) as a good example of a theorist who perceives Black culture in terms of deviance and pathology. A Swedish social scientist, Gunnar Myrdal (1944), also is cited as reflecting the pathology view. He described Black culture as a distorted, pathological condition of the general American culture (p. 225).

Chimezie observes that the focus on pathology, distortion, and failure in describing Black culture is a function of four possible factors: "the unwillingness to admit that Blacks are not whites—physically, psychologically, or culturally; the theorists' inability to break loose from the clutches of his own values; the white myth that Blacks are characterologically deficient; and sociopolitical motivation (the blame the victim orientation)" (p. 226).

I firmly located myself within the camp of the African heritage theorists. The scholarship supporting the other theories is generally sparse and inconclusive. Unfortunately, this has not prevented scholars and policymakers from injecting a negative Black cultural perspective into their work, as we have seen. It is clear that a great deal more work is also needed to continue development of the African heritage theory. Fortunately, historians, anthropologists, political scientists, and art historians have been active in producing research supporting the view that Afro-American culture is based on a strong African heritage.

The African heritage emphasis appeals to me also because it seems to be foundational, chronologically exhaustive, rich, and heuristic. Using Africa as a beginning point for analyzing Black culture creates the broadest possible base for examining the expressions and development of Black culture in the New World.

One misimpression of the earlier edition of this work was that I advocate lower standards or a different educational track for Black children in terms of academic content and/or rigor. Nothing is further from the truth. I advocate the same high educational standards for Black children that are desired for white children. I am seeking to show that we may need to take a different route toward achieving those standards in Black children than is taken in an educational system geared to the learning styles of white children. The schools do a reasonably good job of educating children who come to school prepared to receive the form of education the schools are prepared to deliver. They are not equipped to educate children who are cut out of a different cloth.

Black children are under tremendous pressure to master aspects of at least two distinct cultures, Afro-American culture and Euro-American culture. They are expected to master aspects of Euro-American culture even when their exposure to it is fragmentary. African-American males are at the greatest disadvantage in the feminine orientation of most elementary school classrooms. Cornbleth and Korth (1980) make the point that, in their study of teacher-student interaction in integrated classrooms, teachers favored the behavior of white females over that of white males, Black females, and Black males. The students they identified as having the least potential as learners were Black males. The behaviors they valued least—those of Black males—were the direct opposites of the behaviors they valued most—those of white females.

This whole question of dual socialization is very complex. This book is an attempt to initiate the search for ways to improve Black children's chances for success. It is designed to elucidate the process of bicultural socialization for Black parents, to educate the gatekeepers in the majority culture about the characteristics of Black culture and its points of conflict with white culture, and to advocate greater flexibility and responsiveness to Black children by the mainstream cultural institutions that have an impact on them. Toward that end, let us examine some theoretical issues in bicultural socialization.

Bicultural Socialization

The bicultural model was set forth by Charles Valentine (1971), in an attempt to further develop the cultural difference perspective. He objected to the inference that minority-group members were socialized in a totally distinct cultural context. He felt this would preclude their functioning within the majority institutions in the society. To more correctly conceptualize the process of culturation, Valentine postulated a dual socialization model for minority groups, consisting of enculturation within their own group as well as socialization within the larger society.

Diane de Anda (1984) notes that "although the bicultural model provides an overall conceptual framework, it offers little information regarding the specific mechanisms through which dual socialization occurs." She sought to further explain the process of bicultural socialization and to account for variations among and within ethnic groups in their degree of biculturalism and successful interactions with mainstream society (pp. 101–2).

De Anda lists six factors that can determine whether a member of an ethnic minority is likely to become bicultural:

1. The degree of overlap or commonality between the two cultures with regard to norms, values, beliefs, perceptions, and the like
2. The availability of cultural translators, mediators, and models
3. The amount and type (positive or negative) of corrective feedback provided by each culture regarding attempts to produce normative behaviors
4. the conceptual style and problem-solving approach of the minority individual and their mesh with the prevalent or valued styles of the majority culture
5. The individual's degree of bilingualism

6. The degree of dissimilarity in physical appearance from the norm in the majority culture, including such traits as skin color and facial features (p. 102).

She suggests that the mixture of these six factors can account for the extent to which an individual is bicultural.

De Anda sees Valentine's model of biculturalism as being two separate cultures, in and out of which the minority individual steps. In her own view, the bicultural experience is possible only because there is overlap between the two cultures. The more overlap there is the more effective is the process of dual socialization.

The melting pot theory of socialization she finds more applicable to European immigrants than to minority groups such as Afro-Americans and Hispanics (she includes Asians, but I believe that their experience has been closer to that of Europeans than to the latter groups). The European immigrants, in contrast to the other groups, had a larger number of shared values and norms. They were better able to conform to a greater number of the cultural expectations of the society into which they had come.

The ability of an individual readily to adjust his behavior to the norms of two cultures depends upon the extent to which these cultures share values and norms for prescribed behaviors. An important factor in the dual socialization process is the amount of conflict there is between the remaining elements that are not shared. There can be some cultural values and beliefs that are mutually exclusive. De Anda cites as an example the "polychronic" view of time in Black and Hispanic cultures (at times referred to as c. p. time, colored people's time). This fluid conception of time may interfere with an individual's functioning in a society where a more structured view of time is the norm.

De Anda also points out that two cultures might not be in opposition but might be applied differently. Complementarity of cultures is as important as similarity (p. 103). Kitano (1969) explains the success of the Japanese in America not by the similarity between Japanese culture and American middle-class culture but by the functional compatibility of the two. Apparently, Japanese-American culture supports success-aspiration and rapid socioeconomic success, but couples these with deference, conformity, and compromise. This combination of values may explain why this group is doing well in America without raising the usual hostility of the mainstream toward participation by minority groups in the security of economic success.*

*It is interesting to note that at the time of this writing (1985) U.S. Congressmen have attacked Japan for imposing import quotas on U.S. products, while Japan enjoys unlimited import privileges to the U.S., and that the response to these attacks was instantaneous conciliation.

Cultural Translators, Mediators, and Models

The availability of certain types of socializing agents can determine the extent to which a person becomes bicultural. De Anda describes the roles of translators, mediators, and models (p. 104).

Translators are members of the minority individual's own ethnic group who have been successful at dual socialization. They are probably the most effective agents of dual socialization. They share their own experiences in negotiating the intricacies of the majority culture and convey ways to meet the society's demands without compromising ethnic values and norms.

Mediators are individuals from mainstream culture who can serve as guides for minority persons. These can be formal socializers such as teachers, counselors, and social workers or informal agents of socialization like peers and mentors. Mediators are not as visible as translators because, not being as familiar with the ethnic culture, they cannot as readily identify points of convergence or divergence between the two cultures. However, they can offer valuable information that the minority person may not have access to on his own.

Models are members of the minority person's ethnic group whose behavior can serve as a pattern to emulate. De Anda suggests that the modeling process can be enhanced by perceived similarity between the model and the individual or the identification of the model as a controller of resources (p. 104).

Corrective Feedback

De Anda emphasizes that "corrective feedback" contributes significantly in helping the minority person learn the new culture. It is important to clarify which behaviors are appropriate to particular situations. The type of feedback that is given affects the individual's progress in mastering mainstream culture. Her analysis has important implications for education, as we see in her explanation of how negative responses can disrupt the socialization process:

1. Overly negative feedback creates stress in the minority individual and interferes with his or her learning process.
2. Disproportionate negative to positive feedback discourages the individual from the socialization task.
3. Negative feedback alone doesn't provide information about appropriate responses.
4. Negative feedback can generate negative feelings toward the socializing agent which can result in withdrawal from the task of socialization (p. 105).

In contrast, De Anda suggests that biculturation will be facilitated by socializing agents who provide corrective feedback that is specific, offer feedback regarding both erroneous and more appropriate behavior, tie the specific information to a general rule for use in future situations, and indicate positive aspects of the individual's performance and use this as a source of motivation for future performance (p. 105).

Problem-Solving Skills

The mesh between the conceptual style of the minority culture and that of the majority culture can affect the degree of bicultural socialization. Diane de Anda agrees with Rosalie Cohen (1969) that the analytical learning style is the dominant cognitive style of mainstream American culture. She implies that users of this style may be at an advantage in achieving bicultural socialization. She states, "This style of organizing experience may also help to alleviate some of the problems engendered by conflict between the two cultures because it permits the individual to compartmentalize behavior and affect, allowing him or her to selectively focus, interpret, and respond to the demands of the specific situation" (p. 106).

De Anda maintains that variations in approaches to problem solving can also determine different levels of bicultural socialization between and within minority groups. Factors in problem solving which might vary are:

1. The clarity with which the minority individual is able to define the socialization tasks or problems posed by a culture, and in particular, the essential components of these tasks
2. The extent of an individual's repertoire of generalized strategies, both rules and operations
3. The ability to generate novel combinations of strategies
4. The ability to carry out the necessary operations
5. The ability to utilize evaluative feedback (p. 106).

Degree of Bilingualism

De Anda points out that competence in the language of a culture is an important contributor to bicultural socialization. An individual who is conversant in the language of the majority culture will have access to a greater number of models and mediators and will be better able to utilize corrective feedback from them (p. 106). She says that most members of minority cultures are not what she calls "coordinate" bilinguals, which means that they display equal facility in both languages, but that most of them can be placed on a continuum from monolingual through various degrees of "subordinate" bilingualism.

The factors of interference and dominance characterize the language of the subordinate bilingual. *Interference* refers to the entrance of elements from one language into a person's use of the other, resulting in a "foreign accent" and in grammatical mistakes. De Anda gives the example of the double negative from Spanish being mistakenly used in English. Another example is the use of the verb *to be* in Black English. *Dominance* indicates a differential degree of competence in the two languages.

Competence in the majority language is a reflection of the degree of socialization of the individual and serves a gatekeeping function in access to higher education. Limitation in vocabulary reduces the chances of understanding information imparted by models and mediators, particularly regarding problem-solving processes within the majority culture. Additionally, limited vocabulary, use of incorrect grammatical structures, and the presence of an accent (like that of Black English) serve to emphasize the dissimilarity of the two cultures and to reinforce the belief that minority individuals cannot achieve competence in mainstream institutions (p. 106). Unfortunately, language is regarded as an indicator of intelligence in our culture. Competence in language is used in forming perceptions of learning potential, perceptions which, when acted upon, can have far-reaching effects on school achievement. Minority group individuals are also at a disadvantage in business because of non-standard language usage.

Appearance

De Anda identifies the dissimilarity of physical appearance between members of the minority and majority cultures as an obstacle to bicultural socialization but observes that generally there is a range of variation in physical appearance within ethnic groups such that some members will be closer in appearance than others to individuals of the majority culture. She sees an "insider/outsider" construct—that those individuals who more closely resemble the majority members are more likely to be privy to situations and conversations that provide information that will promote upward mobility. Such a person even has a greater opportunity to be an anonymous observer, as in a large department store. She states: "Not only are these individuals treated similarly to members of the majority culture, but they also can be exposed to disparaging remarks about members of their own ethnic group. Although such an experience produces conflicting emotions for the individual, it also offers information that is not usually available to minority-group members, particularly regarding specific behaviors or beliefs that conflict with mainstream cultural norms" (p. 107).

The issue of appearance is critical in documenting that the oppression of Black people has been more severe than that of other ethnic groups in America. If a graded continuum of appearance characteristics were constructed, we would have to concede that the most valued physical characteristics in America have been keen facial features, fair skin, blue eyes, and blond, straight, long hair. Black (African) people have more of the polar opposites of those features than any other ethnic group—broad facial features, dark skin, dark eyes, and dark, kinky, short hair. Even though other ethnic groups fall at various points on the continuum, because they have varying combinations of the "less desirable" physical features, Black people are clearly most at risk to be oppressed because of differences in appearance.

Even within the Black group, physical dissimilarity from the majority cultural norm is a factor. Those Americans of African descent whose physical appearance is more African suffer more oppression and receive less support generally than their Anglo-appearing peers. This advantage is not as trivial as overhearing conversations, either.

First of all, advantageous physical appearance was rewarded during slavery because it represented bloodline connection with the slaveowner, which usually resulted in differentiation and privilege (house/field distinction). There was also a tendency for slaveowners to provide higher educational opportunities for their slave offspring, which created a privileged mulatto class. An examination of the photographs of Black graduates of Yale University in the latter part of the 19th century reveals a composite of men who look as white as the Ku Klux Klan!

There has been a tendency among Blacks in America since slavery for accomplished men who are dark in skin color to marry fair-skinned women, resulting in offspring who illustrate and perpetuate the association between fair skin and upper social status. In the Black community it has been less common for a very dark-skinned woman to marry a fair-skinned man. The most common occurrence is for a brown-skinned woman to be coupled with a man who is her own color or darker. Some Black men even assert that they would not consider marrying a woman darker than they, so firm is the internalization of the values of the majority in the minds of the minority. This attitude is painful to examine, but we must pinpoint and document the factors that contribute to the continued oppression of the masses of Black people.

De Anda suggests ways in which professionals can assist a minority client in the complex process of dual socialization, hoping to help the individual acquire the information and skills to interact with mainstream institutions while retaining the ability to participate in his own ethnic culture. Her suggestions include:

1. Determining areas of interface between the two cultures that can serve as "doorways" between them

2. Noting the major points of conflict between cultures and the negative consequences for the client
3. Finding and making available translators, mediators, and models who can provide guidelines for dealing with such conflicts and offer critical experiential information
4. Arranging, when possible, for increased corrective feedback for the client in the environment
5. Working to expand the client's repertoire of problem-solving skills, particularly those that are the least context bound, and helping to develop a larger repertoire of context-specific problem-solving skills
6. Educating people of the majority culture about the significant characteristics, values, and needs of minority cultures, as well as serving as advocates of greater flexibility and adjustment in the mainstream culture's institutions.

If this volume has been successful in developing the argument that there is a distinctive Black culture (whatever its source) and if there is support for the theory that minority group members must be socialized in (at least) two cultures, then empirical delineation of this process is clearly called for.

V. P. Franklin,* of Yale University, has stated that

culture does not "cause" an individual to act or react in a given manner, it shapes and guides his or her behavior and also serves as a yardstick or measurement for judging the correctness or appropriateness of a given action. The process of learning cultural values, beliefs, and practices is "acculturation," and it generally takes place in the family and community. The process of learning societal rules, regulations, and social practices is referred to as "socialization," and it generally takes place in the schools and workplace (and in society at large).

The question for which there is presently a lack of empirical evidence is, When is the acculturation offered by the Black family serving to undercut the socialization offered by the American mainstream institutions? Franklin points out that Black family acculturation mechanisms have clearly contributed to the survival of Black people. One clear example is that Black families have protected the self-concepts of Black children by counteracting the negative stereotypes perpetuated by the white-dominated communications media. (It is unfortunate that they could not also prevent the absorption of those stereotypes by whites who are in a position to oppress Black people on the basis of them.)

---

*Personal correspondence June 1984.

Franklin acknowledges that, in the past, Afro-American parents were unable to prevent the cultivation of those negative images by the media, but recently through greater control of educational programs that affect their children, they have pressured the institutions that socialize their children to better represent Black beliefs and values. He affirms the validity of those cultural values: "After all, this was the cultural value system that allowed Afro-Americans to survive the holocaust of American slavery and to advance themselves in a society geared toward keeping Blacks 'in their place.' Afro-Americans have a vested interest in making sure 'socialization' (or integration) does not undo the positive work accomplished through acculturation."

Franklin asserts that Afro-American culture is a very complex set of beliefs and practices. He points out the need to identify cultural diversity within a unified cultural system. He states, "There is no one way of teaching 'Black children' to read, but some methods will have more success because they are embedded in an Afro-American cultural system." I am in agreement with his assertion that "the potential for diversity in responses to educational stimuli is as great among Afro-Americans as any other group of children, and we must always be aware ultimately that each child must be viewed as an individual capable of any number of responses."

The argument of this book for an educational process that is sensitive to Black culture is in no way intended to ignore the diversity of Afro-American children. It is intended as a first step in pointing scholars and educators toward cultural elements in education that may create success for Black children and success for white children. If as many resources could be directed to the exploration of this perspective as have been directed to compensatory education, a perspective advocated by many white social scientists, our evidence would be more definitive.

The time has come in our history for Black scholars to be supported financially in researching and demonstrating culturally based solutions to our problems. Hakim Rashid (1980) asserts that, whereas approximately 25 percent of social science studies deal with minority groups, only about 5 percent of the funds to conduct these studies went to minority researchers. He describes the relationship between Euro-American researchers and Afro-American communities as reflecting a kind of domestic colonialism. I agree with his assertion that African-American researchers in both Black and white institutions must begin to receive research funds at a rate more reflective of the amount of research conducted in Black communities. I have been invited by school districts and governmental agencies throughout the United States to offer my analysis of the achievement gap between Black and white children in the form of consultations, speeches, and in-service training, but *funds* for systematic empirical development of my perspective have not been forthcoming.

Early Childhood Education as Cultural Transition

Hakim Rashid (1981) has pointed out that early childhood education can play an important role in fostering biculturalism in African-American children. However, the "intervention" strategies of the 1960s are passé. He states, "If African-American children are no longer to be viewed as culturally or cognitively deprived, then they must be seen as members of a culture endowed with specific modes of cognition" (p. 59). Early childhood education must search for cultural continuity, not intervention. Rashid states further: "The preschool experience must, therefore, provide a dynamic blend of African-American culture and that culture which is reflected in the Euro-American educational setting. . . . The African-American child who only sees the Euro-American cultural tradition manifested in the preschool environment can only conclude that the absence of visual representations of his culture connotes his essential worthlessness" (p. 60).

There is a need to articulate a pedagogy that includes an environment drawn from African-American culture, teaching strategies embedded in African-American learning styles, and materials relevant to the African-American experience. There should be no "Negro History Corner" or "Negro History Week." There should be an integration of African-American culture in all of its diversity throughout the curriculum.

A companion part of this pedagogy should place an emphasis on language, cognitive skills, and assessment. Early childhood education, though still a very young field, is moving to a level of sophistication in which it is not enough to recite the global goals for children that are beginning to sound like platitudes. The decade of the 1980s is the achievement decade. There is a push for accountability in education. With the recognition of how much young children desire stimulation and how much they are capable of learning has come a companion push for early childhood education to justify itself. We have the technology to promote intellectual development in young children in age-appropriate ways. It is the goal of my current work to further develop this theory of an educational process embedded in Black culture and to move from theory to practice.

The schools, for cultural and educational reasons, need to be pressed to accommodate the learning styles of Black children. Also, Black parents need more information about precisely what skills are required for Black children to perform well on the achievement/

Young children are eager for stimulation and have great capability for learning.

intelligence measures that too often become only instruments of oppression of Black children.

When to fight the system (as in the intelligence test industry) and when to redouble our efforts to prepare Black children to compete in it is a delicate question. It is one to which the Black community must respond. Perhaps there will be no monolithic response from the community as a whole; perhaps the response will be made by each family for its own children as they try to carve out a meaningful balance between assimilation and self-determination. My work is not designed to make that decision. It is intended to provide Black parents and teachers with access to specific ways to facilitate improvement of the language, memory, and reasoning skills that are measured on conventional assessment instruments.

The question of whether America needs an educational process for every ethnic group is not one I feel compelled to answer. Perhaps the answer lies with each ethnic group. I can only affirm the need for a distinctive pedagogy for African Americans. Once such a pedagogy is articulated, I am certain that it can be implemented in a multicultural setting.

However, Black children are at present clustered in about twenty urban school districts throughout the country, because of defacto segregation. These constitute an abundance of already existing sites for research of educational strategies effective in educating Black children. Consequently, the search for an effective pedagogy for Black children need not be interpreted as espousal of either segregation or integration. It does not matter what Blacks espouse. As long as white parents do not want integration, they will continue to send their children to separate or segregated schools. (A trend potentially threatening to Black children is programs for gifted students, which in some schools is resulting in Black children on one floor of the school and white children on another, supposedly in service to giftedness.) Very little real integration has occurred in this country in the thirty years since the 1954 *Brown v. The Board of Education* Supreme Court decision. While some of us struggle for integration, others of us need to get on with the business of creating quality public and private education for Black children.

Bibliography

Abrahams, Roger D. 1970. "Can you dig it?" Aspects of the African esthetic in Afro-American. Paper presented at African Folklore Institute, Indiana University.

Ainsworth, M.D. 1967. *Infancy in Uganda: Infant care and the growth of love.* Baltimore: Johns Hopkins Press.

Akbar, Na'im. 1975. Address before the Black Child Development Institute annual meeting, October 1975, San Francisco.

Almy, M. 1967. Spontaneous Play: An avenue for intellectual development. *Young Children* 22:264–77.

Anderson, Vivian. 1975. A comparison of the sociodramatic play ability of high socioeconomic status Black kindergarten children and high socioeconomic status white kindergarten children. ERIC ED 108 736, National Institute of Education, Washington, D.C.

Baratz, S. S. and J. C. 1969. Negro ghetto children and urban education: A cultural solution. *Social Education* 33:400–404.

Baumrind, Diana. 1972. An exploratory study of socialization effects on Black children: Some Black-white comparisons. *Child Development* 74:261–67.

Bell, R. R. 1965. Lower-class Negro mothers' aspirations for their children. *Social Forces* 43:493–500.

Bell, Robert. 1971. The relative importance of mother and wife roles among Negro lower-class women. In *The Black family: Essays and studies*, ed. Robert Staples. Belmont, Calif.: Wadsworth Press.

Bettelheim, Bruno. 1971. What happens when a child plays? *Ladies Home Journal* 88:34.

Billingsley, Andrew. 1968. *Black families in white America.* New York: Prentice-Hall.

Blassingame, John W. 1972. *The slave community: Plantation life in the antebellum South.* New York: Oxford University Press.

Bohannon, Paul. 1964. *Africa and Africans.* Garden City, N.Y.: American Museum Science Books.

Borg, Walter R. and Gall, Meredith. 1971. *Educational research: An introduction.* New York: David McKay Co.

Borneman, Ernest. 1959. The roots of jazz. In *Jazz*, ed. Nat Hentoff and Albert J. McCarthy. New York: Rinehart and Co.

200

Borowitz, G. H. and others. 1970. Play behavior and competence in ghetto four-year-olds. *Journal of Special Education* 4:215-21.

Borowitz, G. H., Costello, C., and Hirsch, Jay. 1972. Clinical observations of ghetto four-year-olds: Organization, involvement, interpersonal responsiveness, and psychosexual content of play. *Journal of Youth and Adolescence* 1:59-69.

Boykin, A. Wade. 1977. Experimental psychology from a Black perspective: Issues and examples. *Final report from the third conference on empirical research in Black psychology*, ed. William Cross, National Institute of Education, Washington, D.C.

———. 1978. Psychological/behavioral verve in academic/task performance: Pre-theoretical considerations. *Journal of Negro Education* 47:343-54.

Brazelton, T., Koslowski, B., and Tronick, E. 1971. Neonatal behavior among urban Zambians and Americans. *Journal of Child Psychiatry* 15:97-107.

Busse, T. V. and others. 1970. Environmentally enriched classrooms and the play behavior of Negro preschool children. *Urban Education* 5:128-40.

Byers, P. and Byers, H. 1972. Nonverbal communication in the education of children. In *Functions of language in the classroom*, ed. C. Cazden, V. John, and D. Hymes. New York: Teachers' College Press, Columbia University.

Chimezie, Amuzie. 1983. Theories of Black culture. *Western Journal of Black Studies* 7:216-28.

Clark, Kenneth. 1965. *Dark ghetto: Dilemmas of social power*. Foreword by Gunnar Myrdal. New York: Harper and Row.

Cohen, Rosalie. 1969. Conceptual styles, culture conflict and nonverbal tests of intelligence. *American Anthropologist* 71:828-56.

Cohen, Rosalie, Fraenkel, Gerd, and Brewer, John. 1968. The language of the hard core poor: Implications for culture conflict. *Sociology Quarterly* 10:19-28.

Cole, M. and others. 1971. *The cultural context of thinking and learning*. New York: Basic Books.

Cornbleth, Catherine and Korth, William. 1980. Teacher perceptions and teacher-student interaction in integrated classrooms. *Journal of Experimental Education*, Summer, pp. 259-63.

Cox, H. 1969. *The feast of fools*. Cambridge: Harvard University Press.

Curry, Nancy. 1971. Consideration of basic issues on play. In *Play: The child strives toward self-realization*, ed. Nancy E. Curry and Sara Arnaud, Washington, D.C.: NAEYC.

Davis, Angela. 1971. Reflections on the Black woman's role in the community of slaves. *Black Scholar*. 3:2-15.

De Anda, Diane. 1984. Bicultural socialization: Factors affecting the minority experience. *Social Work*, March–April, pp. 101-7.

Dill, Bonnie Thornton. 1980. The means to put my children through: Child-rearing goals and strategies among Black female domestic servants. In *Black woman*, ed. L. Rogers-Rose, pp. 107-24. Beverly Hills, Calif.: Sage Publications.

Dixon, Vernon J. and Foster, Badi G. 1971. *Beyond Black or white.* Boston: Little, Brown.

Dodson, Jualynne. 1975. Final report of black child development project 1975, HEW Office of Child Development, Washington, D.C.

Dubois, W. E. Burghart. 1899. The function of the Negro Church. *The Philadelphia Negro.* Philadelphia: University of Pennsylvania.

————. 1957. *The ordeal of Mansart.* New York: Mainstream.

————. 1961. *The souls of Black folk.* Originally written 1903. Greenwich, Conn.: Fawcett Publications.

Ebsen, Akpan. 1973. The care syndrome: A resource for counseling in Africa. *Journal of Negro Education* 42:205-11.

Eder, P. 1972. Deference behavior in play group situations: A plea for segregated education. *Urban Education* 7:49-65.

Ellison, James. 1984. The seven frames of mind. *Psychology Today,* June, pp. 21-26.

Fine, Elsa. 1973. *The Afro-American artist.* New York: Holt, Rinehart and Winston.

Flavell, J. H. 1963. *The developmental psychology of Jean Piaget.* Princeton: Van Nostrand.

Fleming, Jacquelyn. 1985. *Blacks in college.* San Francisco: Jossey-Bass.

Franklin, John Hope. 1974. *From slavery to freedom: A history of Negro Americans.* New York: Alfred A. Knopf.

Franklin, V. P. 1974. Slavery, personality and Black culture. *Phylon* 35.

————. 1984. *Black self-determination: A cultural history of the faith of the fathers.* Westport, Conn.: Lawrence Hill and Co.

Frazier, E. Franklin. 1964. *The Negro church in America.* New York: Schocken Books.

Friere, Paulo. 1968. *Pedagogy of the oppressed.* New York: Herder and Herder.

Gardner, Howard. 1983. *Frames of mind: The theory of multiple intelligences.* New York: Basic Books.

Geber, Marcelle. 1958. The psycho-motor development of African children in the first year, and the influence of maternal behavior. *Journal of Social Psychology* 47:185-95.

Geber, Marcelle and Geber, Dean R. 1957. Gesell tests on African children. *Pediatrics* 20:4055.

————. 1958. Psychomotor development in African children: The effects of social class and the need for improved tests. *Bulletin of the World Health Organization* 18:471-76.

Giovanni, Jeanne M. and Billingsley, Andrew. 1970. Child neglect among the poor: A study of parental adequacy in families of three ethnic groups. *Child Welfare* 49:196-204.

Gitter, A., Black, George H., and Mostofsky, David I. 1972. Race and sex in perception of emotion. *Journal of Social Issues* 28:63-78.

Goldman, R. and Sanders, J. 1969. Cultural factors and hearing. *Exceptional Children* 35:489-90.

202

Green, Helen Bagenstose. 1971. Socialization values in West African, Negro and East Indian cultures: A cross-cultural comparison. *Journal of Cross-Cultural Psychology* 2:309–12.

Guttentag, M. 1972. Negro-white differences in children's movement. *Perceptual and Motor Skills* 35:435–36.

Guttentag, M. and Ross, Sylvia. 1972. Movement responses in simple concept learning. *American Journal of Orthopsychiatry* 42:657–65.

Hale, Janice. 1974. A comparative study of the racial attitudes of Black children who attend a pan-African and a non-pan-African preschool. Ph.D. diss., Georgia State University.

———. 1977a. The woman's role: The strength of Black families. *First World: An International Journal of Black Thought* 1:28–30.

———. 1977b. De-mythicizing the education of Black children. *First World: An International Journal of Black Thought* 1:30–35.

———. 1980. The socialization of Black children. *Dimensions* 9:43–48.

———. 1981. Black children: Their roots, culture, and learning styles. *Young Children*, January 36:37–50.

Hannerz, U. 1974. Research in the Black ghetto: A review of the sixties. *Journal of Asian and African Studies* 9:139–59.

Haskins, James and Butts, Hugh F. 1973. *The psychology of Black language*. New York: Barnes and Noble.

Havighurst, Robert J. 1976. The relative importance of social class and ethnicity in human development. *Human Development* 19:56–64.

Henderson, Donald H. 1967. A study of the effects of family structure and poverty on Negro adolescents from the ghetto. Ph.D. diss., University of Pittsburgh.

Henderson, Donald H. and Washington, Alfonzo G. 1975. Cultural differences and the education of Black children: An alternative model for program development. *Journal of Negro Education* 44:353–60.

Herskovits, M. J. 1936. Significance of West Africa for Negro research. *Journal of Negro History* 21:15–30.

———. 1938–39. The ancestry of the American Negro. *American Scholar* 8:84–94.

———. 1951. Present status and needs of Afro-American research. *Journal of Negro History* 36:123–47.

———. 1958. *Myth of the Negro past*. Boston: Beacon Press.

Hill, Robert. 1972. *The strengths of Black families*. New York: Emerson Hall.

———. 1981. The economic status of Black Americans. In *The state of Black America*. New York: National Urban League.

Hilliard, Asa. 1976. Alternatives to IQ testing: An approach to the identification of gifted minority children. Final report to the California State Department of Education.

Holt, J. 1964. *How children fail*. New York: Dell.

Hovey, Richard L. 1971. Cognitive style in African cultures: The global-articulated dimension. Ph.D. diss., Michigan State University.

Jefferson, Sharon. 1985. Few Blacks succeed in Shaker schools. *Cleveland Call and Post*, June 20, 1985, page 16B.

Johnson, Leanor B. 1978. The search for values in Black family research. In *The Black family*, ed. Robert Staples. Belmont, Calif.: Wadsworth Publishing Co.

Johnson, N. J. and Sanday, R. R. 1971. Subcultural variations in an urban poor population. *American Anthropologist* 73:128–43.

Kagan, Jerome, Moss, Howard A., and Siegel, Irving E. 1963. Psychological significance of styles conceptualization. In *Basic cognitive process in children*. Society for Research in Child Development Monograph 86. Chicago: University of Chicago Press.

Kitano, Harry H. L. 1969. *Japanese Americans: The evaluation of a subculture*. Englewood Cliffs, N.J.: Prentice Hall.

Kochman, Thomas. "Fighting words" Black and white. Unpublished paper, University of Illinois, Chicago.

———. 1969. Rapping in the ghetto. In *Black experience: soul*, ed. Lee Rainwater, pp. 51–76. New Brunswick, N.J.: Transaction Books, 1973.

Ladner, Joyce. 1971. *Tomorrow's tomorrow: The Black woman*. Garden City, N.Y.: Doubleday.

Leichter, Hope J. 1973. The concept of educative style. *Teacher's College Record* 75:239–50.

Lein, Laura. 1975. Black American migrant children: Their speech at home and school. *Council on Anthropology and Education Quarterly* 6:1–11.

Lester, Julius. 1969. *Look out Whitey! Black Power's gon' get your mama!* New York: Grove Press.

Levine, Lawrence W. 1977. *Black culture and Black consciousness*. New York: Oxford University Press.

Lewis, Samella. 1978. *Art: African-American*. New York: Harcourt, Brace, Johanovich.

Lieberman, S. and Carter, D. K. 1979. Making it in America: Differences between Black and white ethnic groups. *American Sociological Review* 44:347–66.

Maehr, M. L. 1974. Culture and achievement motivation. *American Psychologist* 29:887–96.

Marans, A. and Lourie, R. 1967. Hypotheses regarding the effects of child-rearing patterns on the disadvantaged child. In *The disadvantaged child*, ed. J. Hellmuth. Seattle: Special Child Publications.

Maslow, A. H. 1968. Some educational implications of the humanistic psychologies. *Harvard Educational Review* 38:1–12.

Massari, David, Hayweiser, L., and Meyer, J. 1969. Activity level and intellectual functioning in deprived preschool children. *Developmental Psychology* 1:286–90.

Mbiti, John S. 1970. *African religions and philosophies*. New York: Anchor.

McAdoo, Harriette. 1979. The extended family kin network and socialization of children in upwardly mobile Black families. *The fourth conference on empirical research in Black psychology,* ed. William E. Cross, Jr. and Algea Harrison, National Institute of Mental Health, Washington, D.C.

Meier, J. H. 1964. Innovations in assessing the disadvantaged child's potential. In *The disadvantaged child,* ed. J. Mellmuth, 1:173–99. New York: Brunner/ Mazel.

Merriam, Alan. 1958. African music. In *Continuity and change in African cultures,* ed. William Bascom and Melville J. Herskovits, Chicago: University of Chicago Press.

Michaels, Sarah. 1980. Sharing time: An oral preparation for literacy. Paper presented at the Ethnography in Education Research Forum, March 1980, University of Pennsylvania, Philadelphia.

Miller, D. 1969. *God and games.* New York: World Publishing Co.

Morgan, Harry. 1976. Neonatal precocity and the Black experience. *Negro Educational Review* 27:129–34.

Moynihan, Daniel P. 1965. *The Negro family: The case for national action.* Washington, D.C.: U.S. Department of Labor.

Mültmann, J., ed. 1971. *Theology of play.* New York: Harper and Row.

Munroe, Robert L., Munroe, Ruth H., and Daniels, Robert E. 1976. Relation of subsistence economy to a cognitive task in two East-African societies. *Journal of Social Psychology* 98:133–34.

Munroe, Robert L. and Munroe, Ruth H. 1977. Cooperation and competition among East-African and American children. *Journal of Social Psychology* 101:145–46.

Munroe, Ruth H. and Munroe, Robert L. 1975. Infant care and childhood performance in East Africa. ERIC ED 115 369, National Institute of Education, Washington, D.C.

Myrdal, Gunnar. 1944. *An American dilemma: The Negro problem and modern democracy,* vol. II. New York: Harper and Brothers.

National Alliance of Black School Educators, Inc. *Saving the African American child.* A report of the NABSE Task Force on Black Academic and Cultural Excellence, Washington, D.C., November 1984.

Neale, R. 1969. *In praise of play.* New York: Harper and Row.

Nedler, Shari E. and McAfee, Oralie D. 1979. *Working with parents.* Belmont, Calif.: Wadsworth Publishing Co.

Newmeyer, J. A. 1970. Creativity and nonverbal communication in preadolescent White and Black children. Ph.D. diss., Harvard University.

Nobles, Wade W. 1974a. African root and American fruit: The Black family. *Journal of Social and Behavioral Sciences,* Spring 1974.

———. 1974b. Africanity: Its role in black families. *Black Scholar.* 5:10–17.

———. 1975. The Black family and its children: The survival of humaneness. Unpublished paper.

Norment, Lynn. 1981. To spank or not to spank is still the question. *Ebony*, October, pp. 51–66.

Nyiti, Raphael M. 1976. The development of conservation in the Meru children of Tanzania. *Child Development* 47:1122–29.

Olmsted, Frederick L. 1860. *A journey in the Black country*. New York: Schocken Books (reprint of 1860 edition).

Otterbein, K. F. and Otterbein, C. S. 1973. Believers and beaters: A case study of supernatural beliefs and child-rearing in the Bahama Islands. *American Anthropologist* 75:1670–71.

Patterson, Orlando. 1972. Rethinking Black history. *African Report* 17:29–31.

Piaget, Jean. 1966. Necessité et signification des rescherches comparatives en psychologie génétique. *International Journal of Psychology* 1:3–13.

Piestrup, Ann. 1974. *Black dialect interference and accommodation of reading instruction in first grade*. Language Behavior Research Laboratory Monographs, vol. 4. Berkeley: University of California.

Polling the children. *Time*, March 14, 1977.

Quarles, Benjamin. 1969. *Frederick Douglass*. New York: Atheneum.

Radin, Norma. 1970. Child-rearing practices and cognitive development in lower-class preschool children. ERIC ED 055 671, National Institute of Education, Washington, D.C.

Rainwater, Lee. 1970. *Behind ghetto walls*. Chicago: Aldine.

Ramirez, Manuel and Price-Williams, Douglas. 1976. Achievement motivation in children of three ethnic groups in the United States. *Journal of Cross-Cultural Psychology* 7:47–60.

Rashid, H. M. 1980. Minorities in educational research. *Communication Quarterly*, Summer.

———. 1981. Early childhood education as a cultural transition for African American children. *Educational Research Quarterly* 6:55–63.

Rohwer, W. and Harris, W. 1975. Media effects on prose learning in two populations of children. *Journal of Educational Psychology* 67:651–57.

Rosen, C. E. 1974. The effects of sociodramatic play on problem-solving behavior among culturally disadvantaged preschool children. *Child Development* 45:920–70.

Salamone, Frank A. 1969. Further notes on Hausa culture and personality. *International Journal of Social Psychiatry* 16:39–44.

Sandis, Eva. 1970. Transmission of mother's educational ambitions as related to specific socialization techniques. *Journal of Marriage and the Family* 32:204–11.

Sarason, S. B. 1973. Jewishness, blackishness, and the nature-nurture controversy. *American Psychologist* 28:962–71.

Scott, Joseph. 1976. Polygamy: A futuristic family arrangement among African Americans. *Black Books Bulletin* 4:13–19.

Shaler, N. S. 1890. Science and the African problem. *Atlantic Monthly* 66:36–45.

Shelton, Austin. 1968. Igbo child-raising, eldership, and dependence: Further notes for gerontologists and others. *Gerontologist* 8:236–41.

Silberman, C. 1970. *Crisis in the classroom.* New York: Vintage Books.

Simmons, Warren. 1979. The role of cultural salience in ethnic and social class differences in cognitive performance. *Final report of the fourth conference on empirical research in Black psychology.* National Institute of Mental Health.

Singleton, John. 1969. Cross-cultural approaches to research on minority group education. ERIC ED 040 245, National Institute of Education, Washington, D.C.

Smitherman, Geneva. 1973. White English in blackface, or who do I be? *Black Scholar,* June 1973.

Staples, Robert. 1974. The Black family revisited: A review and a preview. *Journal of Social and Behavioral Sciences* 20:65–78.

———. 1976. *Introduction to Black sociology.* New York: McGraw-Hill Book Co.

Stewart, James B. 1980. Perspectives on Black families from contemporary soul music: The case of Millie Jackson. *Phylon* 41:57–71.

Stodolsky, S. S. and Lesser, Gerald S. 1967. Learning patterns in the disadvantaged. *Harvard Educational Review* 37:546–93.

Sutton-Smith, B. 1967. Role of play in cognitive development. *Young Children* 22:360–70.

———. 1972. Play as a transformational set. *Journal of Health, Physical Education and Recreation* 43:25–54.

Textor, Robert. 1967. *A cross-cultural summary.* New Haven: HRAF Press.

Thurman, Howard. 1980. *The centering moment.* San Francisco: Friends United.

Tillman, James A., Jr. and Tillman, Mary N. 1969. *Why America needs racism and poverty.* Washington, D.C.: Limited Edition publication.

Turner, James. 1971. Black studies and a Black philosophy of education. *Imani,* August/September 1971, pp. 12–17.

UNICEF. 1974. The development of scientific and mathematical thinking among African children. Report of conference sponsored by UNICEF in Sierra Leone, West Africa.

Valentine, Charles A. 1968. *Culture and Poverty.* Chicago: University of Chicago Press.

———. 1971. Deficit, difference and bicultural models of Afro-American behavior, *Harvard Educational Review* 41:137–57.

Wachs, T., Uzgiris, I., and Hunt, J. M. 1971. Cognitive development in infants of different age levels and from different environmental backgrounds: An explanatory investigation. *Merrill Palmer Quarterly* 17:283–316.

Wade-Gayles, Gloria. 1980. She who is Black and mother: In sociology and fiction, 1940–70. In *The Black woman,* ed. Lafrances Rodgers-Rose. Beverly Hills Calif.: Sage.

Ward, T. 1973. Cognitive processes and learning: Reflections on a comparative study of cognitive style (Witken) in fourteen African societies. *Comparative Education Review* 17:1–10.

Webber, Thomas C. 1978. *Deep like the rivers*. New York: Norton Publishing Co.

Williams, Robin. 1964. *Strangers next door*. Englewood Cliffs, N.J.: Prentice-Hall.

Witken, H. A. 1967. A cognitive-style approach to cross-cultural research. *International Journal of Psychology*. 2:237–38.

Woodson, Carter G. 1933. *The miseducation of the Negro*. Washington, D.C.: Associated Press.

Young, Virginia H. 1970. Family and childhood in a southern Georgia community. *American Anthropologist* 72:269–88.

Zigler, E., Abelson, W., and Seitz, V. 1972. Motivational factors in the performance of economically disadvantaged children on the Peabody Picture Vocabulary Test. *Child Development* 44:294–303.

Zigler, E. and Butterfield, E. 1968. Motivational aspects of changes in IQ test performance of culturally deprived nursery school children. *Child Development* 39:1–14.

Index

Janice E. Hale-Benson was born in Fort Wayne, Indiana, and educated in the public schools of Columbus, Ohio. She received a B.A. degree in sociology and elementary education from Spelman College and a masters in religious education from the Interdenominational Theological Center, Atlanta, Georgia. She earned a Ph.D. in early childhood education from Georgia State University. Her postdoctoral work has included travel to West Africa to study African life and culture.

Dr. Hale-Benson is associate professor of early childhood education at Cleveland State University and is founder and executive director of Visions for Children, an early childhood program designed to implement the theories described in *Black Children*.

Dimensions, a journal of the Southern Association on Children Under Six, for information in the article, "The Socialization of Black Children" by Janice Hale, in Vol. 9, No. 1 (October 1980), pp. 43–48. Reprinted by permission of *Dimensions*.

Young Children, a journal of the National Association for the Education of Young Children, for information in the article, "Black Children: Their Roots, Culture, and Learning Styles" by Janice Hale, in Vol. 36, No. 2 (January 1981), pp. 37–50. Copyright 1981. Reprinted by permission of *Young Children*.

Harper and Row Publishers for the first stanza of "Heritage" from *On These I Stand* by Countee Cullen, copyright 1925 by Harper and Row Publishers, renewed 1953 by Ida M. Cullen. Reprinted by permission of the publisher.

Alfred A. Knopf, Inc. for "Mother to Son" and "Note on Commercial Theatre" from *Selected Poems of Langston Hughes*, copyright 1926 by Alfred A. Knopf and renewed 1954 by Langston Hughes. Reprinted by permission of the publisher.

Ronald Coleman, 120–25 Benchley Place, Bronx, New York 10475, for "I Ask You, My Children," printed in the 1977 calendar of the National Black Child Development Institute.